Christmas,
1992

To Joyce

I called the
Presbyterian Minister
to ask what to give
to a Newly Ordained
Elder — and he
said "This is the
book!"
Love
Dad and Mother

A Long Obedience in the Same Direction

Discipleship in an Instant Society

Eugene H. Peterson

InterVarsity Press
Downers Grove
Illinois 60515

For Lu and Peter
companions in the long obedience

● 1980 by Inter-Varsity Christian Fellowship of the United States of America.

InterVarsity Press is the book-publishing division of InterVarsity Christian Fellowship, a student movement active on campus at hundreds of universities, colleges and schools of nursing in the United States of America, and a member movement of the International Fellowship of Evangelical Students. For information about local and regional activities, write Public Relations Dept., InterVarsity Christian Fellowship, 6400 Schroeder Rd., P.O. Box 7895, Madison, WI 53707-7895.

Biblical quotations, unless otherwise noted, are from The Revised Standard Version of the Bible, copyrighted 1946, 1952 ● 1971, 1973, and are used by permission.

Prayer #15 in Little Prayers and Finite Experience by Paul Goodman. Volume Twenty-Four of The Religious Perspective Series edited by Ruth Nanda Anshen. Copyright © 1972 by The Estate of Paul Goodman. Reprinted by permission of Harper and Row, Publishers, Inc.

ISBN 0-87784-727-4
Library of Congress Catalog Card Number: 79-2715

Printed in the United States of America

24	23	22	21	20	19	18	17	16	15	14
02	01	00	99	98	97	96	95	94	93	92

1: Discipleship

"How Will You Compete with Horses?"

If you have raced with men on foot, and they have wearied you, how will you compete with horses?

Jeremiah 12:5

The essential thing "in heaven and earth" is . . . that there should be long obedience in the same direction; there thereby results, and has always resulted in the long run, something which has made life worth living.

Friedrich Nietzsche, *Beyond Good and Evil*

This world is no friend to grace. A person who makes a commitment to Jesus Christ as Lord and Savior does not find a crowd immediately forming to applaud the decision nor old friends spontaneously gathering around to offer congratulations and counsel. Ordinarily there is nothing directly hostile, but an accumulation of puzzled disapproval **and** agnostic indifference constitutes, nevertheless, surprisingly formidable opposition.

An old tradition sorts the difficulties we face in the life of faith into the categories of world, flesh and devil.[1] We are, for the most part, well warned of the perils of the flesh and the wiles of the devil. Their temptations have a definable shape and maintain an historical continuity. That doesn't make them any easier to resist; it does make them easier to recognize.

The world, though, is protean: each generation has the world to deal with in a new form. *World* is an atmosphere, a mood.[2] It is nearly as hard for a sinner to recognize the world's temptations as it is for a fish to discover impurities in the water. There is a sense, a feeling, that things aren't right, that the environment is not whole, but just what it is eludes analysis. We know that the spiritual atmosphere in which we live erodes faith, dissipates hope and corrupts love, but it is hard to put our finger on what is wrong.

Tourists and Pilgrims

One aspect of *world* that I have been able to identify as harmful to Christians is the assumption that anything worthwhile can be acquired at once. We assume that if something can be done at all, it can be done quickly and efficiently. Our attention spans have been conditioned by thirty-second commercials. Our sense of reality has been flattened by thirty-page abridgments.

It is not difficult in such a world to get a person interested in the message of the gospel; it is terrifically difficult to sustain the interest. Millions of people in our culture make decisions for Christ, but there is a dreadful attrition rate. Many claim to have been born again, but the evidence for mature Christian discipleship is slim. In our kind of culture anything, even news about God, can be sold if it is packaged freshly; but when it loses its novelty, it goes on the garbage heap. There is a great market for religious experience in our world; there is little enthusiasm for the patient acquisition of virtue, little inclination to sign up for a long apprenticeship in what earlier generations of Christians called holiness.

Religion in our time has been captured by the tourist mindset. Religion is understood as a visit to an attractive site to be made when we have adequate leisure. For some it is a weekly jaunt to church. For others, occasional visits to special services. Some, with a bent for religious entertainment and sacred diversion, plan their lives around special events like retreats, rallies and conferences. We go to see a new personality, to hear a new truth, to get a new experience and so, somehow, expand our otherwise humdrum lives. The religious life is defined as the latest and the newest: Zen, faith-healing, human potential, parapsychology, successful living, choreography in the chancel, Armageddon. We'll try anything—until something else comes along.

I don't know what it has been like for pastors in other cultures and previous centuries, but I am quite sure that for a pastor in Western culture in the latter part of the twentieth century the aspect of *world* that makes the work of leading Christians in the way of faith most difficult is what Gore Vidal has analyzed as "today's passion for the immediate and the casual."[3] Everyone is in a hurry. The persons whom I lead in worship, among whom I counsel, visit, pray, preach, and teach, want short cuts. They want me to help them fill out the form that will get them instant credit (in eternity). They are impatient for results. They have adopted the lifestyle of a tourist and only want the high points. But a pastor is not a tour guide. I have no interest in telling apocryphal religious stories at and around dubiously identified sacred sites. The Christian life cannot mature under such conditions and in such ways.

Friedrich Nietzsche, who saw this area of spiritual truth, at least, with great clarity wrote, "The essential thing 'in heaven and earth' is . . . that there should be long obedience in the same direction; there thereby results, and has always resulted in the long run, something which has made life worth living."[4] It is this "long obedience in the same direction" which the mood of the world does so much to discourage.

In going against the stream of the world's ways there are two biblical designations for people of faith that are extremely useful: *disciple* and *pilgrim. Disciple (mathetes)* says we are people who spend our lives apprenticed to our master, Jesus Christ. We are in a growing-learning relationship, always. A disciple is a learner, but not in the academic setting of a schoolroom, rather at the work site of a craftsman. We do not acquire information about God but skills in faith.

Pilgrim (parepidemos) tells us we are people who spend our lives going someplace, going to God, and whose path for getting there is the way, Jesus Christ. We realize that "this world is not my home" and set out for the "Father's house." Abraham, who "went out," is our archetype. Jesus, answering Thomas' question, "Lord, we do not know where you are going; how can we know the way?" gives us directions: "I am the way, and the truth, and the life; no one comes to the Father, but by me" (Jn. 14:5-6). The letter to the Hebrews defines our program: "Therefore, since we are surrounded by so great a cloud of witnesses, let us lay aside every weight, and sin which clings so closely, and let us run with perseverance the race that is set before us, looking to Jesus the pioneer and perfecter of our faith" (Heb. 12:1-2).

A Dog-eared Songbook

In the pastoral work of training people in discipleship and accompanying them in pilgrimage, I have found, tucked away in the Hebrew Psalter, an old dog-eared songbook. I have used it to provide continuity in guiding others in the Christian way, and directing people of faith in the conscious and continuous effort which develops into maturity in Christ. The old songbook is called, in Hebrew, *šire hamm'elot*—the Songs of Ascents. The songs are the psalms numbered 120 through 134 in the book of Psalms.

These fifteen psalms were likely sung, possibly in sequence, by Hebrew pilgrims as they went up to Jerusalem to the great worship festivals. Jerusalem was the highest city geographically in Palestine, and so all who traveled there spent much of their time ascending.[5] But the ascent was not only literal, it was also a metaphor: the trip to Jerusalem acted out a life lived upward toward God, an existence that advanced from one level to another in developing maturity. What Paul described as "the upward call of God in Christ Jesus" (Phil. 3:14).

Three times a year faithful Hebrews made that trip (Ex. 23:14-17; 34:22-24). The Hebrews were a people whose salvation had been accomplished in the exodus, whose identity had been defined at Sinai and whose preservation had been assured in the forty years of wilderness wandering. As such a people they regularly climbed the road to Jerusalem to worship. They refreshed their memories of God's saving ways at the Feast of Passover in the

spring; they renewed their commitments as God's cov-
enanted people at the Feast of Pentecost in early summer;
they responded as a blessed community to the best that God
had for them at the Feast of Tabernacles in the autumn.
They were a redeemed people, a commanded people, a
blessed people. These foundational realities were preached
and taught and praised at the annual feasts. Between
feasts the people lived these realities in daily discipleship
until the time came to go up to the mountain city again as
pilgrims to renew the covenant.

This picture of the Hebrews singing these fifteen psalms
as they left their routines of discipleship and made their
way from towns and villages, farms and cities, as pilgrims
up to Jerusalem has become embedded in the Christian de-
votional imagination. It is our best background for understanding life as a faith-journey.

We know that our Lord from a very early age "went up"
to Jerusalem for the annual feasts (Lk. 2:41-42). We continue to identify with the first disciples who "were on the
road, going up to Jerusalem, and Jesus was walking ahead
of them; and they were amazed, and those who followed
were afraid" (Mk. 10:32). We also are amazed and afraid
for there is wonder upon unexpected wonder on this road,
and there are fearful specters to be met. Singing the fifteen
psalms is a way both to express the amazing grace and to
quiet the anxious fears.

There are no better "songs for the road" for those who
travel the way of faith in Christ, a way that has so many con-
tinuities with the way of Israel. Since many (not all) essential
items in Christian discipleship are incorporated in these
songs, they provide a way to remember who we are and
where we are going. I have not sought to produce scholarly
expositions of these psalms but to offer practical medita-
tions which use these tunes for stimulus, encouragement
and guidance. If we learn to sing them well, they can be

a kind of vade mecum for a Christian's daily walk.

Between the Times

Paul Tournier, in *A Place for You,* describes the experience of being in between—between the time we leave home and arrive at our destination; between the time we leave adolescence and arrive at adulthood; between the time we leave doubt and arrive at faith.[6] It is like the time when a trapeze artist lets go the bars and hangs in midair, ready to catch another support: it is a time of danger, of expectation, of uncertainty, of excitement, of extraordinary aliveness.

Christians will recognize how appropriately these psalms may be sung between the times: between the time we leave the world's environment and arrive at the Spirit's assembly; between the time we leave sin and arrive at holiness; between the time we leave home on Sunday morning and arrive in church with the company of God's people; between the time we leave the works of the law and arrive at justification by faith. They are songs of transition, brief hymns that provide courage, support and inner direction for getting us to where God is leading us in Jesus Christ.

Meanwhile the world whispers, "Why bother? There is plenty to enjoy without involving yourself in all that. The past is a graveyard; ignore it; the future is a holocaust; avoid it. There is no payoff for discipleship; there is no destination for pilgrimage. Get God the quick way; buy instant charisma." But other voices speak, if not more attractively, at least more truly. Thomas Szasz, in his therapy and writing, has attempted to revive respect for what he calls the "simplest and most ancient of human truths: namely, that life is an arduous and tragic struggle; that what we call 'sanity'—what we mean by 'not being schizophrenic'—has a great deal to do with competence, earned by struggling for excellence; with compassion, hard won by confronting conflict; and with modesty and patience, acquired through silence and suffering."[7] His testimony validates the decision of those who commit themselves to explore the world of the Psalms of Ascents, who mine them for wisdom and sing them for cheerfulness.

These psalms were no doubt used in such ways by the multitudes Isaiah described as traveling "up to the mountain of the LORD, to the house of the God of Jacob; that he may teach us his ways and that we may walk in his paths" (Is. 2:3). They are also evidence of what Isaiah promised when he said, "You shall have a song as in the night when a holy feast is kept; and gladness of heart, as when one sets out to the sound of the flute to go to the mountain of the LORD, to the Rock of Israel" (Is. 30:29).

Everyone who travels the road of faith requires assistance from time to time. We need cheering up when spirits flag; we need direction when the way is unclear. One of Paul Goodman's "little prayers"[8] expresses our needs,

On the highroad to death
trudging, not eager to get
    to that city, yet the way is
    still too long for my patience

—teach me a travel song,
Master, to march along
    as we boys used to shout
    when I was a young scout.

For those who choose to live no longer as tourists, but as pilgrims, the Psalms of Ascents combine all the cheerfulness of a travel song, with the practicality of a guidebook and map. Their unpretentious brevity is excellently described by William Faulkner. "They are not monuments, but footprints. A monument only says, 'At least I got this far,' while a footprint says, 'This is where I was when I moved again.' "[9]

2: Repentance

"Woe Is Me, that I Sojourn in Meshech"

In my distress I cry to the LORD,
  that he may answer me:
"Deliver me, O LORD,
  from lying lips,
  from a deceitful tongue."

What shall be given to you?
  And what more shall be done to you,
  you deceitful tongue?
A warrior's sharp arrows,
  with glowing coals of the broom tree!

Woe is me, that I sojourn in Meshech,
  that I dwell among the tents of Kedar!
Too long have I had my dwelling
  among those who hate peace.
I am for peace;
  but when I speak,
  they are for war!

Psalm 120

**Before a man can do things there
must be things he will not do.**

Mencius

People submerged in a culture swarming with lies and malice feel like they are drowning in it: they can trust nothing they hear, depend on no one they meet. Such dissatisfaction with the world as it is is preparation for traveling in the way of Christian discipleship. The dissatisfaction, coupled with a longing for peace and truth, can set us on a pilgrim path of wholeness in God.

A person has to be thoroughly disgusted with the way things are to find the motivation to set out on the Christian way. As long as we think that the next election might eliminate crime and establish justice or another scientific breakthrough might save the environment or another pay raise might push us over the edge of anxiety into a life of tranquillity, we are not likely to risk the arduous uncertainties of the life of faith. A person has to get fed up with the ways of the world before he, before she, acquires an appetite for the world of grace.

Psalm 120 is the song of such a person, sick with the lies and crippled with the hate, a person doubled up in pain over what is going on in the world. But it is not a mere outcry, it is pain that penetrates through despair and stimulates a new beginning—a journey to God which becomes a life of peace.

The fifteen Psalms of Ascents describe elements common to all those who apprentice themselves to the Lord Christ and who travel in the Christian way. This first of them is the prod which gets them going. It is not a beautiful song—there is nothing either hauntingly melancholy nor lyrically happy in it. It is harsh. It is discordant. But it gets things started.

Lies without Error

In my distress is the opening phrase. The last word is *war*. Not a happy song, but an honest and necessary one.

Men are set against each other. Women are at each other's throats. We are taught rivalry from the womb. The world is restless, always spoiling for a fight. No one seems to know how to live in healthy relationships. We persist in turning every community into a sect, every enterprise into a war. We realize, in fugitive moments, that we were made for something different and better—"I am for peace"—but there is no confirmation of that realization in our environment, no encouragement of it in our experience. "I am for peace; but when I speak, they are for war!"

The distress that begins and ends the song is the painful awakening to the no longer avoidable reality that we have been lied to. The world, in fact, is not as it has been represented to us. Things are not all right as they are, and they are not getting any better.

We have been told the lie ever since we can remember: that human beings are basically nice and good. Everyone is born equal and innocent and self-sufficient. The world is a pleasant, harmless place. We are born free. If we are in chains now, it is someone's fault, and we can correct it with just a little more intelligence or effort or time.

How we can keep on believing this after so many centuries of evidence to the contrary is difficult to comprehend, but nothing we do or nothing anyone else does to us seems to disenchant us from the spell of the lie. We keep expecting things to get better, somehow. And when they don't we whine like spoiled children who don't get their way. We accumulate resentment that stores up in anger and erupts in violence. Convinced by the lie that what we are experiencing is unnatural, an exception, we devise ways to escape the influence of what other people do to us by getting away on a vacation as often as we can. When the vacation is over we get back into the flow of things again, our naiveté renewed that everything is going to work out all right—only to once more be surprised, hurt, bewildered when it doesn't. The lie ("everything is O.K.") covers up and perpetuates the deep wrong, disguises the violence, the war, the rapacity.

Christian consciousness begins in the painful realization that what we had assumed was the truth is in fact a lie. Prayer is immediate: "Deliver me, O LORD, from lying lips, from a deceitful tongue." Rescue me from the lies of advertisers who claim to know what I need and what I desire, from the lies of entertainers who promise a cheap way to joy, from the lies of politicians who pretend to instruct me in power and morality, from the lies of psychologists who offer to shape my behavior and my morals so that I will live long, happily and successfully, from the lies of religionists who "heal the wounds of this people lightly," from the lies of moralists who pretend to promote me to the office of captain of my fate, from the lies of pastors who "leave the commandment of God, and hold fast the tradition of men" (Mk. 7:8). Rescue me from the person who tells me of life and omits Christ, who is wise in the ways of the world and ignores the movement of the Spirit.

The lies are impeccably factual. They contain no errors. There are no distortions or falsified data. But they are lies all the same because they claim to tell us who we are and omit everything about our origin in God and our destiny in God. They talk about the world without telling us that God made it. They tell us about our bodies without telling us that they are temples of the Holy Spirit. They instruct us in love without telling us about the God who loves us and gave himself for us.

Lightning Illuminating the Crossroads
The single word *LORD* occurs only once in this psalm, but it

is the clue to the whole. God, once admitted to the consciousness, fills the entire horizon. God, revealed in his creative and redemptive work, exposes all the lies. The moment the word *God* is uttered, the world's towering falsehood is exposed—we see the truth. The truth about me is that God made and loves me. The truth about those sitting beside me is that God made them and loves them, and that each one is therefore my neighbor. The truth about the world is that God rules and provides for it. The truth about what is wrong with the world is that I and the neighbor sitting beside me have sinned in refusing to let God be for us, over us and in us. The truth about what is at the center of our lives and of our history is that Jesus Christ was crucified on the cross for our sins and raised from the tomb for our salvation and that we can participate in new life as we believe in him, accept his mercy, respond to his love, attend to his commands.

John Baillie wrote, "I am sure that the bit of the road that most requires to be illuminated is the point where it forks."[1] The psalmist's LORD is a lightning flash illuminating just such a crossroads. Psalm 120 is the decision to take one way as over against the other. It is the turning point marking the transition from a dreamy nostalgia for a better life to a rugged pilgrimage of discipleship in faith, from complaining about how bad things are to pursuing all things good. This decision is said and sung on every continent in every language. The decision has been realized in every sort of life in every century in the long history of mankind. The decision is quietly (and sometimes not so quietly) announced from thousands of Christian pulpits all over the world each Sunday morning. The decision is witnessed by millions in homes, factories, schools, businesses, offices and fields every day of every week. The people who make the decision and take delight in it are the people called Christians.

A No That Is a Yes

The first step toward God is a step away from the lies of the world. It is a renunciation of the lies we have been told about ourselves and our neighbors and our universe. "Woe is me, that I sojourn in Meshech, that I dwell among the tents of Kedar! Too long have I had my dwelling among those who hate peace." Meshech and Kedar are place names: Meshech a far-off tribe, thousands of miles from Palestine in southern Russia; Kedar a wandering Bedouin tribe of barbaric reputation along Israel's borders. They represent the strange and the hostile. Paraphrased, the cry is, "I live in the midst of hoodlums and wild savages; this world is not my home and I want out."

The usual biblical word describing the no we say to the world's lies and the yes we say to God's truth is *repentance*. It is always and everywhere the first word in the Christian life. John the Baptist's preaching was, "Repent, for the kingdom of heaven is at hand" (Mt. 3:2). Jesus' first preaching was the same: "Repent, for the kingdom of heaven is at hand" (Mt. 4:17). Peter concluded his first sermon with "Repent, and be baptized" (Acts 2:38). In the last book of the Bible the message to the seventh church is "be zealous and repent" (Rev. 3:19).

Repentance is not an emotion. It is not feeling sorry for your sins. It is a decision. It is deciding that you have been wrong in supposing that you could manage your own life and be your own god; it is deciding that you were wrong in thinking that you had, or could get, the strength, education and training to make it on your own; it is deciding that you have been told a pack of lies about yourself and your neighbors and your world. And it is deciding that God in Jesus Christ is telling you the truth. Repentance is a realization that what God wants from you and what you want from God are not going to be achieved by doing the same old things, thinking the same old thoughts. Repentance is a decision to follow Jesus Christ and become his pilgrim in the path of peace.

Repentance is the most practical of all words and the most practical of all acts. It is a feet-on-the-ground kind of word. It puts a person in touch with the reality which God creates. Elie Weisel, in referring to the stories of the Hasidim, says that in the tales by Israel of Rizhim one motif comes back again and again: a traveler loses his way in the forest; it is dark and he is afraid. Danger lurks behind every tree. A storm shatters the silence. The fool looks at the lightning, the wise man at the road that lies—illuminated—before him.[2]

Whenever we say no to one way of life that we have long been used to, there is pain. But when the way of life is, in fact, a way of death, a way of war, the quicker we leave it the better. There is a condition that sometimes develops in our bodies called adhesions—parts of our internal organs become attached to other parts. The condition has to be corrected by a surgical procedure—a decisive intervention. The procedure hurts, but the results are healthy. As the Jerusalem Bible puts verses 3-4, "How will he [God] pay back the false oath of a faithless tongue? With war arrows hardened over red-hot charcoal!" Emily Dickinson's spare sentence is an epigraph: "Renunciation—the piercing virtue!"

God's arrows are judgments aimed at provoking repentance. The pain of judgment, called down against the evil-doers could turn them also from their deceitful and violent ways to join our pilgrim on the way of peace. Any hurt is worth it that puts us on the path of peace, setting us free for the pursuit, in Christ, of eternal life. It is the action that follows the realization that history is not a blind alley, and guilt not an abyss. It is the discovery that there is always a way that leads out of distress—a way that begins in repentance, or turning to God. Whenever we find God's people

living in distress there is always someone who provides this
hope-charged word, showing the reality of a different day:
"In that day there will be a highway from Egypt to Assyria,
and the Assyrian will come into Egypt, and the Egyptian into Assyria, and the Egyptians will worship with the Assyr-
ians" (Is. 19:23-25). All Israel knew of Assyria was war—the
vision shows them at worship. Repentance is the catalytic
agent for the change. Dismay is transformed into what a
later prophet would describe as gospel.

The whole history of Israel is set in motion by two such
acts of world rejection, which freed the people for an af-
firmation of God: "the rejection of Mesopotamia in the
days of Abraham and the rejection of Egypt in the days of
Moses."[3] All the wisdom and strength of the ancient world
was in Mesopotamia and Egypt. But Israel said no to it.
Despite the prestige, the vaunted and uncontested greatness, there was something foundationally alien and false in
those cultures: "I am for peace; but when I speak, they are
for war!" Mesopotamian power and Egyptian wisdom were
strength and intelligence divorced from God, put to the
wrong ends and producing all the wrong results.

Modern interpretations of history are variations on the
lies of the Mesopotamians and Egyptians in which, as Abraham Heschel describes it, "man reigns supreme, with the
forces of nature as his only possible adversaries. Man is
alone, free, and growing stronger. God is either nonex-
istent or unconcerned. It is human initiative that makes history, and it is primarily by force that constellations change.
Man can attain his own salvation."[4]

So Israel said no and became a pilgrim people, picking
a path of peace and righteousness through the battlefields
of falsehood and violence, finding a path to God through
the labyrinth of sin.

We know that Israel, in saying that no, did not miracu-
lously return to Eden and live in primitive innocence, or

mystically inhabit a heavenly city and live in supernatural ecstasy. They worked and played, suffered and sinned in the world as everyone else did, and as Christians still do. But they were now *going* someplace—they were going to God. The truth of God explained their lives, the grace of God fulfilled their lives, the forgiveness of God renewed their lives, the love of God blessed their lives. The no released them to a freedom that was diverse and glorious. The judgment of God invoked against the people of Meshech and Kedar was, in fact, a sharply worded invitation to repentance, asking them to join in the journey.

Among the more fascinating pages of American history are those that tell the stories of the immigrants to these shores in the nineteenth century. Thousands upon thousands of people, whose lives in Europe had become mean and poor, persecuted and wretched, left. They had heard of a place where a new start could be made. They had gotten reports of a land where the environment was a challenge instead of an oppression. The stories continue to be told in many families, keeping alive the memory of the event that made an American out of what was a German or an Italian or Scot.

My grandfather left Norway eighty years ago in the midst of a famine. His wife and ten children remained behind until he could return and get them. He came to Pittsburgh and worked in the steel mills for two years until he had enough money to go back and get his family. When he returned with them he didn't stay in Pittsburgh although it had served his purposes well enough the first time, but he traveled on to Montana, plunging into new land, looking for a better place.

In all these immigrant stories there are mixed parts of escape and adventure; the escape from an unpleasant situation; the adventure of a far better way of life, free for new things, open for growth and creativity. Every Christian has some variation on this immigrant plot to tell.

"Woe is me, that I sojourn in Meshech, that I dwell among the tents of Kedar! Too long have I had my dwelling among those who hate peace." But we don't have to live there any longer. Repentance, the first word in Christian immigration, sets us on the way to traveling in the light. It is a rejection that is also an acceptance, a leaving that develops into an arriving, a no to the world that is a yes to God.

3: Providence

"Keep You from All Evil"

I lift up my eyes to the hills.
  From whence does my help come?
My help comes from the LORD,
  who made heaven and earth.

He will not let your foot be moved,
  he who keeps you will not slumber.
Behold, he who keeps Israel
  will neither slumber nor sleep.

The LORD is your keeper;
  the LORD is your shade
  on your right hand.
The sun shall not smite you by day,
  nor the moon by night.

The LORD will keep you from all evil;
  he will keep your life.
The LORD will keep
  *your **going** out and your coming in*
  from this time forth and for evermore.

Psalm 121

But to deviate from the truth for the sake of some prospect of hope of our own can never be wise, however slight that deviation may be. It is not our judgement of the situation which can show us what is wise, but only the truth of the Word of God. Here alone lies the promise of God's faithfulness and help. It will always be true that the wisest course for the disciple is always to abide solely by the Word of God in all simplicity.

Dietrich Bonhoeffer

The moment we say no to the world and yes to God all our problems are solved, all our questions answered, all our troubles over. Nothing can disturb the tranquility of the soul at peace with God. Nothing can interfere with the blessed assurance that all is well between me and my Savior. Nothing and no one can upset the enjoyable relationship which has been established by faith in Jesus Christ. We Christians are among that privileged company of persons who don't have accidents, who don't have arguments with our spouses, who aren't misunderstood by our peers, whose children do not disobey us.

If any of those things should happen—a crushing doubt, a squall of anger, a desperate loneliness, an accident that puts us in the hospital, an argument that puts us in the doghouse, a rebellion that puts us on the defensive, a misunderstanding that puts us in the wrong—it is a sign that something is wrong with our relationship with God. We have, consciously or unconsciously, retracted our yes to God; and God, impatient with our fickle faith, has gone off to take care of someone more deserving of his attention.

Is that what you believe? If it is, I have some incredibly good news for you. You are wrong.

To be told we are wrong is sometimes an embarrassment, even a humiliation. We want to run and hide our heads in shame. But there are times when finding out we are wrong is sudden and immediate relief, and we can lift up our heads in hope. No longer do we have to keep doggedly trying to do something that isn't working.

A few years ago I was in my backyard with my lawn mower tipped on its side. I was trying to get the blade off so that I could sharpen it. I had my biggest wrench attached to the nut, but couldn't budge it. I got a four-foot length of pipe and slipped it over the wrench handle to give me leverage, and was leaning on that—still unsuccessfully. Next I took a large rock and was banging on the pipe. By this time I was beginning to get emotionally involved with my lawn mower. Then my neighbor walked over and said that he had a lawn mower like mine once and that, if he remembered correctly, the threads on the bolt went the other way. I reversed my exertions and, sure enough, the nut turned easily. I was glad to have been wrong. I was saved from frustration and failure. I would never have gotten the job done, no matter how hard I tried, doing it my way.

Psalm 121 is a quiet voice, gently and kindly telling us that we are, perhaps, wrong in the way we are going about the Christian life, and then, very simply, showing us the right way. As such it is the necessary sequel to the previous psalm which gets us started on the Christian way. It put a name to the confused and bewildering feelings of alienation and distrust that made us dissatisfied and restless in a way of life that ignores or rejects God, and prodded us into the repentance that renounces the "devil and all his works" and affirms the way of faith in Jesus Christ.

But no sooner have we plunged, expectantly and enthusiastically, into the river of Christian faith than we get our noses full of water and come up coughing and choking. No sooner do we confidently stride out on to the road of faith than we trip on an obstruction and fall to the hard surface, bruising our knees and elbows. For many, the first great surprise of the Christian life is in the form of troubles we meet. Somehow it is not what we had supposed: we had expected something quite different; we had our minds set on Eden or on New Jerusalem. We are rudely awakened to something very different and we look around for help, scanning the horizon for someone who will give us aid: "I lift up my eyes to the hills. From whence does my help come?"

Psalm 121 is the neighbor coming over and telling us that we are doing it the wrong way, looking in the wrong place for help. Psalm 121 is addressed to those of us who, "disregarding God, gaze to a distance all around them, and make long and devious circuits in quest of remedies to their troubles."[1]

Travelers' Advisory

Three possibilities for harm to travelers are referred to in the psalm. A person traveling on foot can, at any moment, step on a loose stone and sprain his ankle. A person traveling on foot, under the protracted exposure to a hot sun, can become faint with sunstroke. And a person traveling for a long distance on foot, under the pressures of fatigue and anxiety, can become emotionally ill, which was described by ancient writers as moonstroke (or by us as *lunacy*).

We can update the list of dangers. Provisions for law and order can break down with dismaying ease: a crazed person with a handgun or piece of explosive can turn the computerized travel plans of three hundred air passengers into instant anarchy. Disease can break through our pharmaceutical defenses and invade our bodies with crippling pain and death. An accident—in an automobile, from a stepladder, on an athletic field—can without warning interrupt our carefully laid plans. We take precautions by learning safety rules, fastening our seat belts and taking out insurance policies. But we cannot guarantee security.

In reference to these hazards the psalm says, "He will not let your foot be moved. . . . The sun shall not smite you by day, nor the moon by night." Are we to conclude then that Christians never sprain their ankles, never get sunstroke, never have any emotional problems? That is what it sounds like. Yet we know plenty of instances to the contrary. Some of the best Christians I know have sprained their ankles, have fainted, have been overwrought with anxiety. Put that way, either I'm wrong (these people I thought were Christians really weren't and therefore the psalm doesn't apply to them) or the psalm is wrong (God doesn't do what the psalm claims).

Help from the Hills?

But neither the psalm nor our experience are so easily disposed of. A psalm which has enjoyed high regard among Christians so long, must have truth in it that is verified in Christian living. Let's return to the psalm: the person set on the way of faith gets into trouble, looks around for help ("I lift up my eyes to the hills") and asks a question: "From whence does my help come?" As this person of faith looks around at the hills for help, what is he, what is she, going to see?

Some magnificent scenery for one thing. Is there anything more inspiring than a ridge of mountains silhouetted against the sky? Does any part of this earth promise more in terms of majesty and strength, of firmness and solidity, than the mountains? But a Hebrew would see something else. During the time this psalm was written and sung, Palestine was overrun with popular pagan worship. Much of this religion was practiced on hilltops. Shrines were set up, groves of trees were planted, sacred prostitutes both male and female were provided; persons were lured to the shrines to engage in acts of worship that would enhance the fertility of the land, would make you feel good, would protect you from evil. There were nostrums, protections, spells and enchantments against all the perils of the road. Do you fear the sun's heat? Go to the sun priest and pay for protection against the sun god. Are you fearful of the malign influence of moonlight? Go to the moon priestess and buy an amulet. Are you haunted by the demons that can use any pebble under your foot to trip you? Go to the shrine and learn the magic formula to ward off the mischief. From whence shall my help come? from Baal? from Asherah? from the sun priest? from the moon priestess?[2]

They must have been a shabby lot: immoral, diseased, drunken—frauds and cheats all. The legends of Baal are full of the tales of his orgies, the difficulty of rousing him out of a drunken sleep to get his attention. Elijah taunting the priests of Baal ("Perhaps he is asleep and must be awakened," 1 Kings 18:27) is the evidence. But shabby or not, they promised help. A traveler in trouble would hear their offer.

That is the kind of thing a Hebrew, set out on the way of faith twenty-five hundred years ago, would have seen on the hills. It is what disciples still see. A person of faith encounters trial or tribulation and cries out, "Help." We lift our eyes to the hills, and offers of help, instant and numerous, appear. "From whence does my help come?" From the hills? No. "My help comes from the LORD, who made heaven and earth."

A look to the hills for help ends in disappointment. For all their majesty and beauty, for all their quiet strength and firmness, they are, finally, just hills. And for all their promises of safety against the perils of the road, for all the allurements of their priests and priestesses, they are, all, finally, lies. As Jeremiah put it: "Truly the hills are a delusion, the orgies on the mountains" (Jer. 3:23).[3]

And so Psalm 121 says no. It rejects a worship of nature, a religion of stars and flowers, a religion that makes the best of what it finds on the hills; instead it looks to the Lord who made heaven and earth. Help comes from the Creator, not from the creation. The Creator is always awake: he will not slumber or sleep. Baal took long naps, and one of the jobs of the priests was to wake him up when someone needed his attention—and they were not always successful. The Creator is Lord over time: he "will keep your going out and your coming in," your beginnings and your endings. He is

with you when you set out on your way; he is still with you
when you arrive at your destination. You don't need to, in
the meantime, get supplementary help from the sun or the
moon. The Creator is Lord over all natural and supernatural forces: he made them. Neither sun, moon nor rocks
have any spiritual power. They are not able to inflict evil
upon us: we need not fear any supernatural assault from
any of them. "The LORD will keep you from all evil."

The promise of the psalm—and both Hebrews and
Christians have always read it this way—is not that we shall
never stub our toes, but that no injury, no illness, no accident, no distress will have evil power over us, that is, will be
able to separate us from God's purposes in us.

No literature is more realistic and honest in facing the
harsh facts of life than the Bible. At no time is there the
faintest suggestion that the life of faith exempts us from
difficulties. What it promises is preservation from all the
evil in them. On every page of the Bible there is recognition
that faith encounters troubles. The sixth petition in the
Lord's Prayer is "Lead us not into temptation, but deliver
us from evil." That prayer is answered every day, sometimes many times a day, in the lives of those who walk in the
way of faith. St. Paul wrote, "No temptation has overtaken
you that is not common to man. God is faithful, and he will
not let you be tempted beyond your strength, but with the
temptation will also provide the way of escape, that you
may be able to endure it" (1 Cor. 10:13).

Five times in Psalm 121 God is referred to by the personal
name *LORD*. Six times he is described as the *keeper*. He is not
an impersonal executive that gives orders from on high; he
is present help every step of the way we travel. Do you think
the way to tell the story of the Christian way is to describe
its trials and tribulations? It is not. It is to name and to describe God who preserves, accompanies and rules us.

All the water in all the oceans cannot sink a ship unless it gets inside. Nor can all the trouble in the world harm us unless it gets within us. That is the promise of the psalm: "The LORD will keep you from all evil." Not the demon in the loose stone, not the fierce attack of the sun god, not the malign influence of the moon goddess—not any of these can separate you from God's call and purpose. From the time of your repentance that got you out of Kedar and Meshech to the time of your glorification with the saints in heaven, you are safe: "The LORD will keep you from all evil." None of the things that happen to you, none of the troubles you encounter, have any power to get between you and God, dilute his grace in you, divert his will from you (see Rom. 8:28, 31-32).

The only serious mistake we can make when illness comes, when anxiety threatens, when conflict disturbs our relationships with others is to conclude that God has gotten bored in looking after us and has shifted his attention to a more exciting Christian, or that God has become disgusted with our meandering obedience and decided to let us fend for ourselves for awhile, or that God has gotten too busy fulfilling prophecy in the Middle East to take time now to sort out the complicated mess we have gotten ourselves into. That is the *only* serious mistake we can make. It is the mistake that Psalm 121 prevents: the mistake of supposing that God's interest in us waxes and wanes in response to our spiritual temperature.

The great danger of Christian discipleship is that we should have two religions: a glorious, biblical Sunday gospel that sets us free from the world, that in the cross and resurrection of Christ makes eternity alive in us, a magnificent gospel of Genesis and Romans and Revelation; and, then, an everyday religion that we make do with during the week between the time of leaving the world and arriving in heaven. We save the Sunday gospel for the big crises of existence. For the mundane trivialities—the times when

our foot slips on a loose stone, or the heat of the sun gets
too much for us, or the influence of the moon gets us down
—we use the everyday religion of the *Reader's Digest* reprint,
advice from a friend, an Ann Landers column, the huck-
stered wisdom of a talk-show celebrity. We practice patent-
medicine religion: we know that God created the universe
and has accomplished our eternal salvation. But we can't
believe that he condescends to watch the soap opera of our
daily trials and tribulations; so we purchase our own remedies for that. To ask him to deal with what troubles us each
day is like asking a famous surgeon to put iodine on a
scratch.

But Psalm 121 says that the same faith that works in the
big things works in the little things. The God of Genesis 1
who brought light out of darkness is also the God of this
day who keeps you from all evil.

Traveling Companion
The Christian life is not a quiet escape to a garden where
we can walk and talk uninterruptedly with our Lord; not a
fantasy trip to a heavenly city where we can compare our
blue ribbons and gold medals with others who have made
it to the winners' circle. To suppose that, or to expect that,
is to turn the nut the wrong way. The Christian life is going
to God. In going to God Christians travel the same ground
that everyone else walks on, breathe the same air, drink the
same water, shop in the same stores, read the same news-
papers, are citizens under the same governments, pay the
same prices for groceries and gasoline, fear the same dangers, are subject to the same pressures, get the same dis-
tresses, are buried in the same ground.

The difference is that each step we walk, each breath we
breathe, we know we are preserved by God, we know we
are accompanied by God, we know we are ruled by God;
and therefore no matter what doubts we endure or what

accidents we experience, the Lord will preserve us from evil, he will keep our life. We know the truth of Luther's hymn: "And though this world, with devils filled, should threaten to undo us, we will not fear, for God hath willed His truth to triumph through us. The prince of darkness grim, we tremble not for him; his rage we can endure, for Lo! his doom is sure; one little word shall fell him." We Christians believe that life is created and shaped by God and that the life of faith is a daily exploration of the constant and countless ways in which God's grace and love are experienced.

Psalm 121, learned early and sung repeatedly in the walk with Christ, clearly defines the conditions under which we live out our discipleship, which, in a word, is God. Once we get this psalm in our hearts it will be impossible for us to gloomily suppose that being a Christian is an unending battle against ominous forces that at any moment may break through and overpower us. Faith is not a precarious affair of chance escape from satanic assaults. It is the solid, massive, secure experience of God who keeps all evil from getting inside us, who keeps our life, who keeps our going out and our coming in from this time forth and forevermore.

4: Worship

"Let Us Go to the House of the LORD!"

I was glad when they said to me,
"Let us go to the house of the LORD!"
Our feet have been standing
within your gates, O Jerusalem!

Jerusalem, built as a city
which is bound firmly together,
to which the tribes go up,
the tribes of the LORD,
as was decreed for Israel,
to give thanks to the name of the LORD.
There thrones for judgment were set,
the thrones of the house of David.

Pray for the peace of Jerusalem!
"May they prosper who love you!
Peace be within your walls,
and security within your towers!"
For my brethren and companions' sake
I will say, "Peace be within you!"
For the sake of the house of the LORD our God,
I will seek your good.

Psalm 122

There is something morally repulsive about modern activistic theories which deny contemplation and recognize nothing but struggle. For them not a single moment has value in itself, but is only a means for what follows.

Nicholas Berdyaev

One of the afflictions of pastoral work has been to listen, with a straight face, to all the reasons people give for not going to church: "My mother made me when I was little." "There are too many hypocrites in the church." "It's the only day I have to sleep in." There was a time when I responded to such statements with simple arguments that exposed them as flimsy excuses. Then I noticed that it didn't make any difference. If I showed the inadequacy of one excuse, three more would pop up in its place. So I don't respond anymore. I listen (with a straight face) and go home and pray that that person will one day find the one sufficient reason for going to church, which is God. I go about my work hoping that what I do and say will be usable by the Holy Spirit to create in that person a determination to worship God in a Christian community.

Many people do: they decide to worship God, faithfully and devoutly. It is one of the important acts in a life of discipleship. And what is far more interesting than the reasons (excuses) people give for not worshiping, is discovering the reasons why they do.

Psalm 122 is the song of a person who decides to go to church and worship God. It is a sample of the complex, diverse and worldwide phenomenon of worship that is common to all Christians. It is an excellent instance of what happens when a person worships.

Psalm 122 is third in the sequence of the Psalms of Ascents. Psalm 120 is the psalm of repentance—the no that gets us out of an environment of deceit and hostility and sets us on our way to God. Psalm 121 is the psalm of trust—a demonstration of how faith resists patent-medicine remedies to trials and tribulations and determinedly trusts God to work out his will and "keep you from all evil" in the midst of difficulty. Psalm 122 is the psalm of worship—an example of what people of faith everywhere and always do: gather to an assigned place and worship their God.

An Instance of the Average

The first line catches many by surprise. "I was glad when they said to me, 'Let us go to the house of the Lord!' " But it shouldn't. Worship is the most popular thing that Christians do. A great deal of what we call Christian behavior has become part of our legal system and is embedded in our social expectations, both of which have strong coercive powers. If we removed all laws from society and eliminated all consequences for antisocial acts, we don't know how much murder, how much theft, how much perjury and falsification would take place. But we do know that much of what we commonly describe as Christian behavior is not volitional at all—it is enforced.

But worship is not forced. Everyone who worships does so because he or she wants to. There are, to be sure, a few temporary coercions—children and spouses who attend church because another has decided that they must. But these coercions are short-lived, a few years at most. Most Christian worship is voluntary. An excellent way to test people's values is to observe what we do when we don't *have* to do anything, how we spend our leisure time, how we spend our extra money. Even in a time when church attendance is not considered to be on the upswing, the numbers are impressive. There are more people at worship on any given Sunday, for instance, than are at all the football games or on the golf links or fishing or taking walks in the woods. Worship is the single most popular act in this land.

So when we hear the psalmist say, "I was glad when they said to me, 'Let us go to the house of the LORD,' " we are not listening to the phony enthusiasm of a propagandist drumming up business for worship; we are witnessing what is typical of most Christians in most places at most times. This is not an exception to which we aspire; it is an instance of the average.

A Framework

Why do we do it? Why is there so much voluntary and faithful worship by Christians? Why is it that we never find a Christian life without, in the background somewhere, an act of worship, never find Christian communities without also finding Christian worship? Why is it that worship is the common background to all Christian existence and that it is so faithfully and willingly practiced? The psalm singles out three items: worship gives us a workable structure for life; worship nurtures our needs to be in relationship with God; worship centers our attention on the decisions of God.

Worship gives us a workable structure for life. The psalm says, "Jerusalem, built as a city which is bound firmly together, to which the tribes go up, the tribes of the LORD." Jerusalem, for a Hebrew was *the* place of worship (only incidentally was it the geographical center of the country and the political seat of authority). The great worship festivals to which everyone came at least three times a year were held in Jerusalem. In Jerusalem everything that God said was remembered and celebrated. When you went to Jerusalem, you encountered the great foundational realities: God created you, God redeemed you, God provided for you. In Jerusalem you saw in ritual and heard proclaimed in preaching the powerful history-shaping truth that God forgives our sins and makes it possible to live without guilt and with purpose. In Jerusalem all the scattered fragments of experience, all the bits and pieces of truth and feeling and perception were put together in a single whole.

The King James Version translates this sentence, "Jerusalem is builded as a city that is compact together." Earlier Coverdale had translated the phrase, "That is at unity with itself." The city itself was a kind of architectural metaphor for what worship is: all the pieces of masonry fit compactly, all the building stones fit harmoniously. There were no loose stones, no leftover pieces, no awkward gaps in the walls or towers. It was well built, compactly built, skillfully built, "at unity with itself."

What is true architecturally is also true socially, for the sentence continues, " . . . to which the tribes go up, the tribes of the LORD." In worship all the different tribes functioned as a single people in harmonious relationship. In worship though we have come from different places and out of various conditions, we are demonstrably after the same things, saying the same things, doing the same things. With all our differing levels of intelligence and wealth, background and language, rivalries and resentments, still, in worship we are gathered into a single whole. Outer quarrels and misunderstandings and differences pale into insignificance as the inner unity of what God builds in the act of worship is demonstrated.

When a person is confused and things refuse to fit together, he sometimes announces a need to get out of the noise and turbulence, to get away from all the hassle and "get my head together." When he succeeds in doing this we call that person "put together." All the parts are there, nothing is left out, nothing is out of proportion, everything fits into a workable frame.

As I entered a home to make a pastoral visit, the person I came to see was sitting at a window embroidering a piece of cloth held taut over an oval hoop. She said, "Pastor, while waiting for you to come I realized what's wrong with me— I don't have a frame. My feelings, my thoughts, my activities—everything is loose and sloppy. There is no border to my life. I never know where I am. I need a frame for my life like this one I have for my embroidery."

How do we get that framework, that sense of solid struc-

ture so that we know where we stand and are therefore able
to do our work easily and without anxiety? Christians go to
worship: week by week we enter the place compactly built,
"to which the tribes go up" and get a working definition for
life: the way God created us, the ways in which he leads us.
We know where we stand.

A Command
Another reason Christians keep returning to worship is
that it nurtures our need to be in relationship with God.
Worship is the place where we obey the command to praise
God: "as was decreed for Israel, to give thanks to the name
of the LORD." This command runs right down the center of
all Christian worship. A decree. A word telling us what we
ought to do; and what we ought to do is praise.

When we sin and mess up our lives, we find that God
doesn't go off and leave us—he enters into our trouble and
saves us. That is good, an instance of what the Bible calls
gospel. We discover reasons and motivations for living in
faith and find that God is already helping us to do it—and
that is good. Praise God! "A Christian," wrote Augustine,
"should be an alleluia from head to foot." That is the reality. That is the truth of our lives. God made us, redeems us,
provides for us. The natural, honest, healthy, logical response to that is praise to God. When we praise we are func-
tioning at the center, we are in touch with the basic, core
reality of our being.

But very often we don't feel like it, and so we say, "It
would be dishonest for me to go to a place of worship and
praise God when I don't feel like it. I would be a hypocrite."
The psalm says, I don't care whether you feel like it or not:
as was *decreed,* "give thanks to the name of the LORD."

I have put great emphasis on the fact that Christians
worship because they want to, not because they are forced
to. But I have never said that we worship because we *feel*

like it. Feelings are great liars. If Christians only worshiped when they felt like it, there would be precious little worship that went on. Feelings are important in many areas, but completely unreliable in matters of faith. Paul Scherer is laconic: "The Bible wastes very little time on the way we feel."[1] We live in what one writer has called the "age of sensation."[2] We think that if we don't *feel* something there can be no authenticity in *doing* it. But the wisdom of God says something different, namely, that we can *act* ourselves into a new way of feeling much quicker than we can *feel* ourselves into a new way of acting. Worship is an *act* which develops feelings for God, not a *feeling* for God which is expressed in an act of worship. When we obey the command to praise God in worship, our deep, essential need to be in relationship with God is nurtured.

A Word of God
A third reason we keep engaging in regular acts of worship is that in it our attention is centered on the decisions of God. Our psalm describes worship as the place where "thrones for judgment were set, the thrones of the house of David." The biblical word *judgment* means "the decisive word by which God straightens things out and puts things right." Thrones of judgment are the places that that word is announced. Judgment is not a word *about* things, describing them; it is a word which *does* things, putting love in motion, applying mercy, nullifying wrong, ordering goodness. This word of God is everywhere in worship. In the call to worship we hear God's first word to us; in the benediction we hear God's last word to us; in the Scripture lessons we hear God speaking to our fathers; in the sermon we hear that word re-expressed to us; in the hymns, which are all to a greater or lesser extent paraphrases of Scripture, the Word of God makes our prayers articulate. Every time we worship our minds are informed, our memories refreshed with

the judgments of God, we are familiarized with what God says, what he has decided, the ways he is working out our salvation.

There is simply no place where these can be done as well as in worship. If we stay at home by ourselves and read the Bible, we are going to miss a lot, for our reading will be unconsciously conditioned by our culture, limited by our ignorance, distorted by unnoticed prejudices. In worship we are part of "the large congregation" where all the writers of Scripture address us, where hymn writers use music to express truths which touch us not only in our heads but in our hearts, where the preacher who has just lived through six days of doubt, hurt, faith and blessing with the worshipers, speaks the truth of Scripture in the language of the congregation's present experience. We want to hear what God says and what he says to us: worship is the place where our attention is centered on these personal and decisive words of God.

Peace and Security

Worship, even for those who are most faithful at it, takes up a small percentage of a person's life, an hour or so a week at most. Does it make any difference to the rest of the week? The final words of Psalm 122 say that it does: "Pray for the peace of Jerusalem! 'May they prosper who love you! Peace be within your walls, and security within your towers!' For my brethren and companions' sake I will say, 'Peace be within you!' For the sake of the house of the LORD our God, I will seek your good." Here we have prayers that overflow the bounds of worship and create new relationships in the city, in society.

The first word, *pray,* is a transition into the everyday world. It is not the word ordinarily used in formal worship, but the everyday Hebrew word for "ask." It is not improperly translated "pray" for when we ask from God we pray. But the asking is not a formal prayer in the sanctuary; it is an informal asking as we go about our business between Sundays. It is the word Hebrews would use to ask for a second helping of potatoes if still hungry, or for directions if lost.

Worship does not satisfy our hunger for God—it whets our appetite. Our need for God is not taken care of by engaging in worship—it deepens. It overflows the hour and permeates the week. The need is expressed in a desire for peace and security. Our everyday needs are changed by the act of worship. We are no longer living from hand to mouth, greedily scrambling through the human rat race to make the best we can out of a mean existence. Our basic needs suddenly become worthy of the dignity of creatures made in the image of God: peace and security. The words *shalom* and *shalvah*, play on the sounds in Jerusalem, *jerushalom*, the place of worship.

Shalom, peace, is one of the richest words in the Bible. You can no more define it by looking up its meaning in the dictionary than you can define a person by his social security number. It gathers all aspects of wholeness that result from God's will being completed in us. It is the work of God that, when complete, releases streams of living water in us and pulsates with eternal life. Every time Jesus healed, forgave or called someone, we have a demonstration of *shalom*.

And *shalvah*, security. It has nothing to do with insurance policies or large bank accounts or stockpiles of weapons. The root meaning is leisure—the relaxed stance of one who knows that everything is all right because God is over us, with us and for us in Jesus Christ. It is the security of being at home in a history that has a cross at its center. It is the leisure of the person who knows that every moment of our existence is at the disposal of God, lived under the mercy of God.

Worship initiates an extended, daily participation in peace and security so that we share in our daily rounds what God initiates and continues in Jesus Christ.

A Pause to Sharpen a Tool

We live in a pragmatic age and are reluctant to do anything if its practical usefulness cannot be demonstrated. It is inevitable that we ask regarding worship, is it worth it? Can you justify the time and energy and expense involved in gathering Christians together in worship? Well, "Look at the mower in the summer's day, with so much to cut down ere the sun sets. He pauses in his labour—is he a sluggard? He looks for his stone, and begins to draw it up and down his scythe, with rink-atink, rink-atink, rink-atink. Is that idle music—is he wasting precious moments? How much he might have mowed while he has been ringing out those notes on his scythe! But he is sharpening his tool, and he will do far more when once again he gives his strength to those long sweeps which lay the grass prostrate in rows before him."[3]

5: Service

"Our Eyes Look to the LORD Our God"

To thee I lift up my eyes,
O thou who art enthroned
in the heavens!
Behold, as the eyes of servants
look to the hand of their master,
as the eyes of a maid
to the hand of her mistress,
so our eyes look to the LORD our God,
till he have mercy upon us.

Have mercy upon us, O LORD, have mercy
upon us,
for we have had more than enough of
contempt.
Too long our soul has been sated
with the scorn of those who are at ease,
the contempt of the proud.

Psalm 123

In general terms, service is a willing, working, and doing in which a person acts not according to his own purposes or plans but with a view to the purpose of another person and according to the

need, disposition, and direction of others. It is an act whose freedom is limited and determined by the other's freedom, an act whose glory becomes increasingly greater to the extent that the doer is not concerned about his own glory but about the glory of the other.... It is *ministerium Verbi divini*, which means, literally, "a servant's attendance on the divine Word." The expression "attendance" may call to mind the fact that the New Testament concept of *Diakonos* originally meant "a waiter." [We] must wait upon the high majesty of the divine Word, which is God himself as he speaks in his action.

Karl Barth

As a person grows and matures in the Christian way, it is necessary to acquire certain skills. One is service. The skill is so difficult to acquire and liable to so many misunderstandings that it is necessary to single it out for special attention from time to time.

Psalm 123 is an instance of service. In this, as so often in the psalms, we are not instructed in what to do, we are provided an instance of what is done. A psalm is not a lecture; it is a song. In a psalm we have the observable evidence of what happens when a person of faith goes about the business of believing and loving and following God. We don't have a rule book defining the action, we have a snapshot of the players playing the game. In Psalm 123 we observe that aspect of the life of discipleship that takes place under the form of a servant.

If God Is God at All
"To thee I lift up my eyes, O thou who art enthroned in the heavens!" Service begins with an upward look to God. God is over us. He is above us. The person of faith looks up to God, not at him or down on him. The servant assumes a certain posture, a stance. If he or she fails to take that posture, attentive responsiveness to the master's commands will be hard.

It is easy to get the wrong idea, for when a person becomes a Christian there is a new sense of confident ability and assured power. Furthermore we are provided promises which tell us to go ahead: "Ask, and it will be given you; seek, and you will find; knock, and it will be opened to you" (Lk. 11:9). God presents himself to us in the history of Jesus Christ as a servant: with that before us it is easy to assume the role of master and begin ordering him around. God is

---

not a servant to be called into action when we are too tired to do something ourselves, not an expert to be called on when we find we are ill equipped to handle a specialized problem in living. Paul Scherer writes scathingly of people who lobby around in the courts of the Almighty for special favors, plucking at his sleeve, pestering him with our requests. God is not a buddy that we occasionally ask to join us at our convenience or for our diversion. God did not become a servant so that we could order him around but so that we could join him in a redemptive lifestyle.

Too often we think of religion as a far-off, mysteriously run bureaucracy to which we apply for assistance when we feel the need. We go to a local branch office and direct the clerk (sometimes called a pastor) to fill out our order for God. Then we go home and wait for God to be delivered to us according to the specifications that we have set down. But that is not the way it works. And if we thought about it for two consecutive minutes, we would not want it to work that way. If God is God at all, he must know more about our needs than we do; if God is God at all, he must be more in touch with the reality of our thoughts, our emotions, our bodies than we are; if God is God at all, he must have a more comprehensive grasp of the interrelations in our families and communities and nations than we do.

"O thou who art enthroned in the heavens!" When the Bible uses that phrase, and it does use it frequently, it is not saying anything about geography or space. Biblical writers are neither geographers nor astronomers—they are theologians. They describe with profound accuracy the relation between God and persons like you and me, a relationship between the Creator and the creature; they coordinate our knowledge of the God who loves us with our experience of being loved; they tell the story of the God who leads us through difficulties and document it with our experience of being guided. We are not presented with a functional god who will help us out of jams or an entertainment god who will lighten tedious hours. We are presented with the God of exodus and Easter, the God of Sinai and Calvary. If we want to understand God, we must do it on his terms. If we want to see God the way he really is, we must look to the place of authority—to Scripture and to Jesus Christ.

And do we really want it any other way? I don't think so. We would very soon become contemptuous of a god whom we could figure out like a puzzle or learn to use like a tool. No, if God is worth our attention at all, he must be a God we can look up to—a God we *must* look up to: "To thee I lift up my eyes, O thou who art enthroned in the heavens!"

The moment we look up to God (and not over at him, or down on him) we are in the posture of servitude.

"Have Mercy upon Me"

A second element in service has to do with our expectation. What happens when we look up to God in faith? There is an awesome mystery in God that we can never completely penetrate. We cannot define God; we cannot package God. But that doesn't mean that we don't know anything about God. It doesn't mean that we are completely at sea with God, never knowing what to expect, nervously on edge all the time, wondering what he might do.

We know very well what to expect, and what we expect is mercy. Three times the expectation is articulated in Psalm 123: "Our eyes look to the LORD our God, till he have mercy upon us. Have mercy upon us, O LORD, have mercy upon us."

The basic conviction of a Christian is that God intends good for us and that he will get his way in us. He does not treat us according to our deserts, but according to his plan. He is not a police officer on patrol, watching over the universe, ready to club us if we get out of hand or put us in jail if we get obstreperous. He is a potter, working with the clay of our lives, forming and reforming until, finally, he has shaped a redeemed life, a vessel fit for the kingdom.

"Have mercy upon us": the prayer is not an attempt to get God to do what he is unwilling, otherwise, to do, but a reaching out to what we know that he does do, an expressed longing to receive what God is doing in and for us in Jesus Christ. In obedience we pray *have mercy upon us* instead of "give us what we want." We pray *have mercy upon us,* and not "reward us for our goodness so our neighbors will acknowledge our superiority." We pray *have mercy upon us* and not "punish us for our badness so we will feel better." We pray *have mercy upon us* and not "be nice to us because we have been such good people."

We live under the mercy. God does not treat us as alien others, lining us up so that he can evaluate our competence or our usefulness or our worth. He rules, guides, commands, loves us as children whose destinies he carries in his heart.

The word *mercy* means that the upward look to God in the heavens does not expect God to stay in the heavens, but to come down, to enter our condition, to accomplish the vast enterprise of redemption, to fashion, in us, his eternal salvation. "The root meaning 'to stoop,' 'to be inclined,' has been conjectured."[1] Servitude is not a vague woolgathering in the general direction of God and not a cringing, cowering terror under the lash of God. Servitude is specific in its expectation, and what it expects is mercy.

Urgent Service
A third element in the servant life is urgency: "Have mercy upon us, for we have had more than enough of contempt. Too long our soul has been sated with the scorn of those who are at ease, the contempt of the proud."

The experience of servitude is recurrent through history. And the experience has never been happy. The psalmist lived in a culture in which the slave and the servant were institutionalized, as they have been at different times in world history. As far as we can tell, it has never worked very well. Power breeds oppression. Masters get lazy and become scornful of those under them. The cry "too long our soul has been sated with the scorn of those who are at ease, the contempt of the proud" is believable. The psalm is part of a vast literature of outcry, a longing for deliverance from oppression.

We live in a similar slavery. True, we have, in our country, abolished the institutionalized forms of slavery and all but eliminated a servant class, but the experience of servitude is still among us and is as oppressive as ever. Freedom is on everyone's lips. Freedom is announced and celebrated. But not many feel or act free. Evidence? We live in a nation of complainers and a society of addicts. Everywhere we turn we hear complaints: I can't spend my money the way I want; I can't spend my time the way I want; I can't be myself; I'm under the control of others all the time. And everywhere we meet the addicts—addiction to alcohol and drugs, to compulsive work habits and to obsessive consumption. We trade masters; we stay enslaved.

The Christian is a person who recognizes that our real problem is not in achieving freedom but in learning service under a better master. The Christian realizes that every relationship that excludes God becomes oppressive. Recognizing and realizing that, we urgently want to live under the mastery of God.

For such reasons all Christian service involves urgency. Servitude is not a casual standing around waiting for orders. It is never desultory; it is urgent need: "Speak Lord, for thy servant hears." And the gospel is the good news that the words of God, commanding new life in us, are already in our ears; "he who has ears to hear, let him hear."

Reasonable Service

The best New Testament commentary on this psalm is in the final section of Paul's letter to the Romans, chapters 12—16. The section begins with this sentence: "I appeal to you therefore, brethren, by the mercies of God, to present your bodies as a living sacrifice, holy and acceptable to God, which is your spiritual worship" (12:1). The psalm's emphasis on actual, physical service (not a spiritual intention, not a desire to be of service) is picked up in the invitation to present our *bodies.* The motivation for service (not coerced, not demanded) is picked up in the phrase "by the mercy." But most significant are the remarkable last two words, *logiken latreian,* which another translation renders "reasonable service." Service, that is, that makes sense. The word *latreia,* means "service," the work one does on behalf of the community. But it also is the base of our word *liturgy,* the service of worship which we render to God. And it is precisely that service that is logical, reasonable. That service we render to God (in worship) is extended into specific acts which serve others. We learn a relationship— an attitude toward life, a stance—of servitude before God, and then we are available to be of use to others in acts of service.

The psalm has nothing in it about serving others. It concentrates on being servant to God. Its position is that if the attitude of servanthood is learned, by attending to God as Lord, then serving others will develop as a very natural way of life. Commands will be heard to be hospitable, to be compassionate, to visit the sick, to help and to heal (commands which Paul assembles in Romans 12—16 and many other places) and carried out with ease and poise.

As we live out the implications of a life of service, we are provided with continuous encouragement and example by Jesus Christ who said, "Do you know what I have done to you? You call me Teacher and Lord; and you are right, for so I am. If I then, your Lord and Teacher, have washed your feet, you also ought to wash one another's feet. For I have given you an example, that you also should do as I have done to you. Truly, truly, I say to you, a servant is not greater than his master; nor is he who is sent greater than he who sent him. If you know these things, blessed are you if you do them" (Jn. 13:12-17).

The Freest Person on Earth

God's people are everywhere and always encouraged to work for the liberation of others, helping to free them from every form of bondage—religious, economic, cultural, political—that sin uses to stunt or thwart or cramp their lives. The promises and fulfillments of freedom are antiphonal throughout Scripture. The glorious theme has extensive documentation in the lives of the people of God. But there are also, sadly, numerous instances in our society of persons who, having been given their freedom, have at once squandered it, using it as "an opportunity for the flesh" (Gal. 5:13), ending in a worse slavery. For freedom is the freedom to live as persons in love for the sake of God and neighbor, not a license to grab and push. It is the opportunity to live at our best, "little less than God" (Ps. 8:5), not as unruly beasts. The work of liberation must therefore be accompanied by instruction in the use of liberty as children of God who "walk by the Spirit" (Gal. 5:25). Those who parade the rhetoric of liberation but scorn the wisdom of service do not lead people into the glorious liberty of the children of God but into a cramped and covetous squalor.

As Psalm 123 prays the transition from oppression ("the contempt of the proud") to freedom ("have mercy upon us") to a new servitude ("as the eyes of servants look to the hand of their master . . . so our eyes look to the LORD"), it puts us in the way of learning how to use our freedom most appropriately, under the lordship of a merciful God.

The consequences are all positive. I have never yet heard a servant Christian complain of the oppressiveness of his servitude. I have never yet heard a servant Christian rail against the restrictions of her service. A servant Christian is the freest person on earth.

6: Help

"We Have Escaped as a Bird from the Snare"

If it had not been the LORD who was on our side,
  let Israel now say—
if it had not been the LORD who was on our side,
  when men rose up against us,
then they would have swallowed us up alive,
  when their anger was kindled against us;
then the flood would have swept us away,
  the torrent would have gone over us;
then over us would have gone
  the raging waters.

Blessed be the LORD,
  who has not given us
  as prey to their teeth!
We have escaped as a bird
  from the snare of the fowlers;
the snare is broken,
  and we have escaped!

Our help is in the name of the LORD,
  who made heaven and earth.

Psalm 124

God is almost intolerably careless about crosses and swords, arenas and scaffolds, about all the "evils" and all the "plagues." His caring doesn't mean that he goes in for upholstering!

Paul Scherer

I was at a Red Cross bloodmobile to donate my annual pint, and being asked a series of questions by a nurse to see if there was any reason for disqualification. The final question on the list was, "Do you engage in hazardous work?" I said, "Yes." She was interrupted from her routine and looked up, a little surprised, for I was wearing a clerical collar by which she could identify me as a pastor. Her hesitation was only momentary: she smiled, ignored my answer and marked the no on her questionaire, saying, "I don't mean *that* kind of hazardous."

I would like to have continued the conversation, comparing what she supposed I meant by hazardous with what I did in fact mean by it. But that was not the appropriate time and place. There was a line of people waiting for their turn at the needle. There are, though, appropriate times and places for just such conversations, and one of them is when Christians encounter Psalm 124. Psalm 124 is a song of hazard—and of help. Among the Psalms of Ascents, sung by **the** people of God on the way of faith, this is one which better than any other describes the hazardous work of all discipleship and declares the help which is always experienced at the hand of God.

A Clerk in the Complaints Department of Humanity

The first lines of the psalm twice describe God as "the LORD who was on our side." The last line is, "Our help is in the name of the LORD, who made heaven and earth." God is on our side. God is our help.

Statements like that are red flags to some people. They provoke challenges. I, confident and assured in the pulpit, can announce, "The Lord is on our side. . . . Our help is in the name of the Lord." But no sooner am I out of the

pulpit than someone is saying to me, "Look, I wish you
would be a little more careful about your pronouns. How
do you get this *our* . . . ? The Lord might be on *your* side,
he might be *your* help. But he is not *mine*. Listen to this. . . . "
Through the week I get case histories of family tragedy
and career disappointment, along with pessimistic re-
counts of world events. The concluding line is a variation
on the theme: "How do you explain that, you who are so
sure that God is on my side?"

I am put on the spot of being God's defender. I am expected to explain God to his disappointed clients. I am
thrust into the role of a clerk in the complaints department
of humanity, asked to trace down bad service, listen sympa-
thetically to aggrieved patrons, try to put right any mistakes
that I can and apologize for the rudeness of the manage-
ment.

But if I accept any of those assignments I misunder-
stand my proper work, for God doesn't need me to defend
him. He doesn't need me for a press secretary, explaining
to the world that he didn't really say what everyone thought
they heard in that interview with Job, or that the quotation
of his word by St. Paul was taken out of context and needs
to be understood against the background paper that Isaiah
wrote.

The proper work for the Christian is witness, not apol-
ogy, and Psalm 124 is an excellent model. It does not argue
God's help; it does not explain God's help; it is a testimony
of God's help in the form of a song. The song is so vigorous, so confident, so bursting with what can only be called
reality, that it fundamentally changes our approach and
our questions. No longer does it seem of the highest prior-
ity to ask, "Why did this happen to me? Why do I feel left
in the lurch?" Instead we ask, "How does it happen that
there are people who sing with such confidence, 'God is our
help'?" The psalm is data that must be accounted for and

the data are so solid, so vital, have so much more substance and are so much more interesting than the other things we hear through the day that it must be dealt with before we can go back to the whimpering complaints.

"If it had not been the LORD who was on our side, let Israel now say—if it had not been the LORD who was on our side, when men rose up against us, then they would have swallowed us up alive, when their anger was kindled against us; then the flood would have swept us away, the torrent would have gone over us; then over us would have gone the raging waters." The witness is vivid and contagious. One person announces the theme, everyone joins in. God's help is not a private experience; it is a corporate reality—not an exception that occurs among isolated strangers, but the norm among the people of God.

God's help is described by means of two illustrations. The people were in danger of being swallowed up alive; and they were in danger of being drowned by a flood. The first picture is of an enormous dragon or sea monster. Nobody has ever seen a dragon, but everybody (especially children) knows they exist. Dragons are projections of our fears, horrible constructions of all that might hurt us. A dragon is total evil. A peasant confronted by a magnificent dragon is completely outclassed. There is no escape: the dragon's thick skin, fiery mouth, lashing serpentine tail, and insatiable greed and lust sign an immediate doom. The second picture, that of the flood, is a picture of sudden disaster. In the Middle East, watercourses which have eroded the countryside are all interconnected by an intricate, gravitational system. A sudden storm fills these little gullies with water, they feed into one another, and in a very few minutes a torrential flash flood is produced. Persons who live in these desert areas are endangered during the rainy season by such unannounced catastrophies. There is no escaping. One minute you are well and happy and making plans for the future; the next minute the entire world is disarranged by a catastrophe.

The psalmist is not a person talking about the good life, how God has kept him out of all difficulty. This person has gone through the worst—the dragon's mouth, the flood's torrent—and finds himself intact. He was not abandoned but helped. The final strength is not in the dragon or in the flood but in "the LORD who was on our side."

We can, of course, avoid dealing with this by employing a cheap back-of-the-hand cynicism. It is inevitable, in one sense, that we should respond with some cynicism to enthusiasm. Advertisers are routinely so dishonest with us that we train ourselves to keep our distance from any who speak with passion and excitement for fear they will manipulate us. We see Pete Rose or Robert Young or Joe Dimaggio speaking on behalf of a product and inwardly discount the witness; we know the words were written by a highly paid copywriter and that the testimonial was done for a handsome fee. In the midst of that kind of world we come on the lines, "If it had not been the LORD who was on our side, when men rose up against us, then they would have swallowed us up alive, . . . " and we say, "Vigorous poetry! Well done! But who was your copywriter, and how much did they pay you to say it?"

The only cure for that kind of cynicism is to bring it out in the open and deal with it. If it is left to work behind the scenes in our hearts, it is a parasite on faith, enervates hope and leaves us anemic in love. Don't hesitate to put the psalm (or any other Scripture passage) under the searchlight of your disbelief! The reason many of us do not ardently believe in the gospel is that we have never given it a rigorous testing, thrown our hard questions at it, faced it with our most prickly doubts.

Subjected to our most relentless and searching criticism, Psalm 124 will, I think, finally convince us of its honesty.

There is no literature in all the world that is more true to life and more honest than the Psalms, for here we have warts-and-all religion. Every skeptical thought, every disappointing venture, every pain, every despair that we can face is lived through and integrated into a personal, saving relationship with God, which relationship also has in it acts of praise, blessing, peace, security, trust and love.

Good poetry survives not when it is pretty or beautiful or nice but when it is true: accurate and honest. The Psalms are great poetry and have lasted not because they appeal to our fantasies and our wishes but because they are confirmed in the intensities of honest and hazardous living. Psalm 124 is not a selected witness, inserted like a commercial into our lives to testify that life goes better with God; it is not part of a media blitz to convince us that God is superior to all the other gods on the market. It is not a press release but honest prayer.

The people who know this psalm best and who have tested it out and used it often (that is, the people of God who are travelers on the way of faith, singing it in all kinds of weather) tell us that it is credible, that it fits into what we know of life lived in faith.

Hazardous Work

Christian discipleship is hazardous work. I hope the Red Cross nurse did not think that I was referring to my pastoral work as hazardous. My work, as such, is no more difficult than anyone else's. Any work done faithfully and well is difficult. It is no harder for me to do my job well than for any other person, and no less. There are no easy tasks in the Christian way; there are only tasks which can be done faithfully or erratically, with joy or resentment. And there is no room for any of us, pastors or grocers, accountants or engineers, typists or gardeners, physicians or teamsters, to speak in tones of self-pity of the terrible burdens of our work.

What is hazardous in my life is my work as a Christian. Every day I put faith on the line. I have never seen God. In a world where nearly everything can be weighed, explained, quantified, subjected to psychological analysis and scientific control I persist in making the center of my life a God whom no eye hath seen, nor ear heard, whose will no one can probe. That's a risk.

Every day I put hope on the line. I don't know one thing about the future. I don't know what the next hour will hold. There may be sickness, personal or world catastrophe. Before this day is over I may have to deal with death, pain, loss, rejection. I don't know what the future holds for me, for those whom I love, for my nation, for this world. Still, despite my ignorance and surrounded by tinny optimists and cowardly pessimists, I say that God will accomplish his will and cheerfully persist in living in the hope that nothing will separate me from Christ's love.

Every day I put love on the line. There is nothing I am less good at than love. I am far better in competition than in love. I am far better at responding to my instincts and ambitions to get ahead and make my mark than I am at figuring out how to love another. I am schooled and trained in acquisitive skills, in getting my own way. And yet, I decide, every day, to set aside what I can do best and attempt what I do very clumsily—open myself to the frustrations and failures of loving, daring to believe that failing in love is better than succeeding in pride.

All that is hazardous work; I live on the edge of defeat all the time. I have never done any one of those things to my (or anyone else's) satisfaction. I live in the dragon's maw and at the flood's edge. "How very hard it is to be/A Christian! Hard for you and me."[1]

The psalm, though, is not about hazards but about help. The hazardous work of discipleship is not the subject of the psalm but only its setting. The subject is help: "Blessed be the LORD, who has not given us as prey to their teeth! We have escaped as a bird from the snare of the fowlers; the snare is broken, and we have escaped! Our help is in the name of the LORD, who made heaven and earth." Hazards or no hazards, the fundamental reality we live with is "The LORD who was on our side. . . . Our help is in the name of the LORD."

When we are first in it, our consciousness of hazard is total: like a bird trapped in a snare. All the facts add up to doom. There is no way out. And then, unaccountably, there *is* a way out. The snare breaks and the bird escapes. Deliverance is a surprise. Rescue is a miracle. "Blessed be the LORD, who has not given us as prey to their teeth!"

How God wants us to sing like this! Christians are not fussy moralists who cluck their tongues over a world going to hell; Christians are people who praise the God who is on our side. Christians are not pious pretenders in the midst of a decadent culture; Christians are robust witnesses to the God who is our help. Christians are not fatigued outcasts who carry righteousness as a burden in a world where the wicked flourish; Christians are people who sing "Blessed be the LORD, who has not given us as prey to their teeth!"

Enlarged Photographs of Ordinary Objects

The final sentence, "Our help is in the name of the LORD, who made heaven and earth," links the God who created heaven and earth to the God who helps us personally. It takes the majesty of the one who pulled a universe into order and beauty, and finds this God involved in the local troubles of a quite ordinary person.

A friend showed me a series of pictures that he had taken. The subject matter consisted exclusively of household items found in an ordinary kitchen: a match stick, a pin, the edge of a knife. Household utensils are not ordinarily thought of as possessing much beauty, but all of these photographs of very ordinary objects were quite astonishingly beautiful. The beauty was suddenly visible because the photographs had all been made through a magnifying lens. Small, ugly, insignificant items were blown into great size and we could see what we had overlooked in our everyday routine. And it turned out that what we had overlooked was careful, planned details which produced exquisite beauty.

I remember particularly well the photograph of a highly magnified brillo pad. Nothing in the kitchen seems quite as ordinary or quite as lacking in aesthetic appeal. When possible we keep them hidden under the sink. No one would think of hanging one on a nail or hook for people to admire. Yet under magnification the brillo pad is one of the most beautiful of kitchen items. The swirl of fine wire is pleasing to the eye. The colors of blue fade in and out of the soap film. What we assume is not worth looking at twice, and best kept in an obscure place, is, on examination, a beautiful construction.

Psalm 124 is a magnification of the items of life that are thought to be unpleasant, best kept under cover, best surrounded with silence lest they clutter our lives with unpleasantness: the dragon's mouth, the flood's torrent, the snare's entrapment; suffering, catastrophe, disaster. They are a very real part of life, and they constitute a dominating, fearful background for many. We look for relief among experts in medicine and psychology, and go to museums to get a look at beauty. Psalm 124 is an instance of a person who digs deeply into the trouble and finds there the presence of the God who is on our side. In the details of the conflict, the majestic greatness of God becomes revealed in the minuteness of a personal history. Faith develops out of the most difficult aspects of our existence, not the easiest. The person of faith is not a person who has been born, luckily, with a good digestion and sunny disposition. The assumption by outsiders that Christians are naive or protected is the opposite of the truth: Christians know more about the deep struggles of life than others, more about the ugliness of sin.

A look into the heavens can bring a breathtaking sense of wonder and majesty, and, if a person is a believer, a feeling of praise to the God who made heaven and earth. The psalm looks the other direction. It looks into the troubles of history, the anxiety of personal conflict and emotional trauma. And it sees there the God who is on our side, God our help. The close look, the microscopic insight into the dragon's terrors, the flood's waters and the imprisoning trap, sees the action of God in deliverance.

We speak our words of praise in a world that is hellish; we sing our songs of victory in a world where things get messy; we live our joy among people who neither understand nor encourage us. But the content of our lives is God, not man. We are not scavenging in the dark alleys of the world, poking in its garbage cans for a bare subsistence. We are traveling in the light, toward God who is rich in mercy and strong to save. It is Christ, not culture, that defines our lives. It is the help we experience, not the hazards we risk, that shape our days.

7: Security

"The LORD Is Round about His People"

Those who trust in the LORD are like Mount Zion,
  which cannot be moved, but abides for ever.
As the mountains are round about Jerusalem,
  so the LORD is round about his people,
  from this time forth and for evermore.
For the scepter of wickedness shall not rest
  upon the land allotted to the righteous,
lest the righteous put forth
  their hands to do wrong.
Do good, O LORD, to those who are good,
  and to those who are upright in their hearts!
But those who turn aside upon their crooked ways
  the LORD will lead away with evildoers!
  Peace be in Israel!

Psalm 125

**Judea was designed to produce in her
inhabitants the sense of seclusion and
security, though not to such a degree
as to relieve them from the attractions of
the great world, which throbbed closely
past, or to relax in them those habits
of discipline, vigilance, and valour,
which are the necessary elements of**

a nation's character. In the position of Judea there was not enough to tempt her people to put their confidence in herself; but there was enough to encourage them to defend their freedom and a strenuous life. And while the isolation of their land was sufficient to confirm their calling to a discipline and destiny separate from other peoples, it was not so complete as to keep them in ignorance of the world or to release them from those temptations to mix with the world, in combating which their discipline and destiny could alone be realised.

George Adam Smith

Climbing is difficult. The tug of gravity is constant. There are barriers to be surmounted and hazards to be met. Ordinarily, though, with a moderate amount of determination and stamina, people complete the climb they begin. But sometimes the foothold gives way and there is a slide backward.

The Rocky Mountains, where our family loves to hike in the summer, are mostly sedimentary rock. There are places where the rock, under the impact of ice and water, erodes to a loose, crumbly stuff called scree. A misstep there can send you cascading down a mountain slope for hundreds of feet.

Backslider was a basic word in the religious vocabulary that I learned as I grew up. *Exempla* were on display throughout the town: people who had made a commitment of faith to our Lord, were active in our little church and who lost their footing on the ascent to Christ and backslid.

My Uncle Harry was a backslider. He was a warm, ardent Christian. In his middle years, on the basis of a mere wisp of rumor, he acquired hundreds of acres of useless land. Not long afterward the Department of Interior decided to build a hydroelectric dam on that land. Suddenly my uncle was a rich man. The excitement of making money got into his blood; attendance at worship became infrequent. He became impatient with his children and with me, his nephew. His work habits became compulsive. That is when I first heard *backslider* applied to someone I knew. He died of high blood pressure and a heart attack. Everyone in his family visibly relaxed.

Two girls, older than I, whom I very much admired, attractive and vivacious, went away to college. They returned for vacation wearing brighter lipstick and shorter skirts.

From the pew in front of me on a Sunday morning I heard the stage whispers between two grandmotherly types: "Do you think they have backslidden?" One is now a pastor's wife near Philadelphia, the other a missionary, with her husband, in Ethiopia.

Backsliding was everywhere and always an ominous possibility. Warnings were frequent and the sad consequences on public display. The mood was anxious and worried. I was taught to take my spiritual temperature every day, or at least every week; if it was not exactly "normal," there was general panic. I got the feeling that backsliding was not something you *did,* it happened to you. It was an accident that intruded on the unwary or an attack that involved the undefended.

Later in life, as I read Scripture for myself, and still later when as a pastor I had the responsibility for guiding the spiritual development of others, I acquired a very different way of looking at the conditions under which the Christian walks the way of discipleship. In both the Scriptures and the pastoral traditions of the church I found a background of confidence, a leisured security, among persons of faith.

Someone Else Built the Fortress

The emphasis of Psalm 125 is not on the precariousness of the Christian life but on its solidity. Living as a Christian is not walking a tightrope without a safety net high above a breathless crowd, many of whom would like nothing better than the morbid thrill of seeing you fall; it is sitting secure in a fortress.

The psalm uses familiar geography to demonstrate the truth: "Those who trust in the LORD are like Mount Zion, which cannot be moved, but abides for ever. As the mountains are round about Jerusalem, so the LORD is round about his people, from this time forth and for evermore."

Jerusalem was set in a saucer of hills. It was the safest of
cities because of the protective fortress these hills provided.
Just so is the person of faith surrounded by the Lord. Better than a city wall, better than a military fortification is the
presence of the God of peace. Geographically the city of
Jerusalem had "borders and bulwarks of extraordinary
variety and intricacy"[1] which illustrated and enforced the
reality of God's secure love and care.

City life in the ancient world was dangerous. The outside
world was filled with roaming marauders, ready to attack
at any sign of weakness. Constant vigilance was a pre-
requisite for community life and for the development of
the arts of civilization. Cities needed elaborate and extensive defense systems to make them safe. An immense
effort was expended on building walls and digging moats.

We still live in that kind of world and we still build those
defenses although the forms have changed somewhat. The
process is not only political but personal. The outer world
is only an extension of an inner, spiritual world. Psychologists who observe us talk of the elaborate security systems
(Sullivan) and the defense mechanisms (Freud) that we use
to protect ourselves.

People of faith have the same needs for protection and
security as anyone else. We are no better than others in
that regard. What is different is that we find that we don't
have to build our own: "God is our refuge and strength, a
very present help in trouble" (Ps. 46:1). "As the mountains
are round about Jerusalem, so the LORD is round about
his people." We don't always have to be looking over our
shoulder lest evil overtake us unawares. We don't always
have to keep our eyes on our footsteps lest we slip, in-
advertently, on a temptation. God is at our side. He is, as
another psalmist put it, "behind and before" (139:5). And
when it comes down to it, do we need anything more than
our Lord's prayer for us: "Holy Father, keep them in thy

name. . . . I do not pray that thou shouldst take them out of the world, but that thou shouldst keep them from the evil one" (Jn. 17:11, 15)? With a prayer like that offered to the Father on our behalf, are we not secure?

A Saw-toothed History

All the same, we do become anxious, we do slip into fearful moods, we become uncertain and insecure. The confident, robust faith that we desire and think is our destiny is qualified by recurrent insecurities. Singing Psalm 125 is one way Christians have to develop confidence and banish insecurity. The psalm makes its mark not by naively whistling when life is dark but by honestly facing the typical insecurities that beset us and putting them in their place.

One threat to our security comes from feelings of depression and doubt. The person of faith is described in this psalm as one who "cannot be moved, but abides for ever." But I am moved. I am full of faith one day and empty with doubt the next. I wake up one morning full of vitality, rejoicing in the sun; the next day I am gray and dismal, faltering and moody. "Cannot be moved"—nothing could be less true of me. I can be moved by nearly anything: sadness, joy, success, failure. I'm a thermometer and go up and down with the weather.

A couple of years ago a friend introduced me to the phrase *the saw-toothed history of Israel.* Israel was up one day and down the next. One day they were marching in triumph through the Red Sea, singing songs of victory, the next they were grumbling in the desert because they missed having Egyptian steak and potatoes for supper. One day they were marching around Jericho blowing trumpets and raising hearty hymns, and the next they were plunged into an orgy at some Canaanite fertility shrine. One day they are with Jesus in the upper room, listening in rapt attention to his commands and receiving his love, the next they are stamping around and cursing in the courtyard, denying they ever knew him.

But all the time, as we read that saw-toothed history, we realize something solid and steady: they are always God's people. God is steadfastly with them, in mercy and judgment, insistently gracious. We get the feeling that everything is done in the sure, certain environment of the God who redeems his people. And as we learn that, we learn to live not by our feelings about God but by the facts of God. I refuse to believe my depressions; I choose to believe in God. If I break my leg I do not become less a person. My wife and children do not repudiate me. Neither when my faith fractures or my feelings bruise does God cast me off and reject me.

My feelings are important for many things. They are essential and valuable. They keep me aware of much that is true and real. But they tell me next to nothing about God or my relation to God. My security comes from who God is, not from how I feel. Discipleship is a decision to live by what I know about God, not by what I *feel* about him or myself or my neighbors. "As the mountains are round about Jerusalem, so the LORD is round about his people." The image that announces the dependable, unchanging, safe, secure existence of God's people comes from geology, not psychology.

A Damoclean Sword

Another source of uncertainty is in our pain and suffering. Unpleasant things happen to us. We lose what we think we cannot live without. Pain comes to those whom we love, and we conclude that there is no justice. Why does God permit this? Anxiety seeps into our hearts. We have the precarious feeling of living under a Damoclean sword. When will the ax fall on me? If such a terrible thing could happen to my friend who is so good, how long until I get mine?

The psalmist knows all this. Sickness and death, despair and persecution. He is familiar with the rape and pillage of military invasion, and the famine and earthquake of natural disaster. Psalm 125 was written by a person who did not have anesthetics in his hospital, aspirin in his medicine chest and whose government did not have hundreds of billions of dollars to spend on national defense. Pain and suffering were most certainly in his daily life. Why did they not destroy his confidence?

The answer is in these words: "For the scepter of wickedness shall not rest upon the land alloted to the righteous, lest the righteous put forth their hands to do wrong." The key word is *rest:* abide there permanently and finally. Israel had more than its share of oppression: the scepter of wickedness was on her time and time again: Pharaoh, the Philistines, Tiglath-Pileser, Sennacherib, Nebuchadnezzar, Caesar. To an outsider it must have looked much of the time as if wicked rule was permanent. From the inside the witness of faith said that it was not: "The scepter of wickedness shall not rest upon the land alloted to the righteous, lest the righteous put forth their hands to do wrong."

If the evil is permanent, if there is no hope for salvation, even the most faithful and devout person will break, " . . . put forth their hands to do wrong." But God does not permit that to happen. Danger and oppression are never too much for faith. They were not too much for Job, they were not too much for Jeremiah and they were not too much for Jesus. Evil is always temporary. "The worst does not last."[2] Nothing counter to God's justice has any eternity to it. Paul's witness was, "God is faithful, and he will not let you be tempted beyond your strength, but with the temptation will also provide the way of escape, that you may be able to endure it" (1 Cor. 10:13). "He knows when to say, It is enough."[3]

A Nonnegotiable Contract

The third threat to the confidence that is promised to the Christian is the known possibility of defection. The general truth under which the Christian lives in this regard is "once saved always saved." Once you are a Christian there is no getting out of it. It is a nonnegotiable contract. Once you have signed you cannot become a free agent again, no matter what the commissioner or the Supreme Court rules.

However true that is generally, and I think it is, there are exceptions. It would seem that if God will not force us to faith in the first place, he will not keep us against our will, finally. Falling away is possible. We know of Judas. We know of Hymenaeus and Alexander who "made shipwreck of their faith" (1 Tim. 1:19-20). These are the ones described in the psalm "who turn aside upon their crooked ways."[4] The way of discipleship gets difficult, they see an opening through the trees that promises a softer, easier path. Distracted and diverted, they leave and never return.

If it is possible to defect, how do I know that I won't— or even worse, that I haven't? How do I know that I have not already lost faith, especially during those times when I am depressed or have one calamity after another piled on me.

Such insinuated insecurities need to be confronted directly and plainly: it is not possible to drift unconsciously from faith to perdition. We wander like lost sheep, true; but he is a faithful shepherd who pursues us relentlessly. We have our ups and downs, zealously believing one day and gloomily doubting the next, but he is faithful. We break our promises, but he doesn't break his. Discipleship is not a contract in which if we break our part of the agreement he is free to break his; it is a covenant in which he establishes the conditions and guarantees the results.

Certainly, you may quit if you wish. You may say no to God. It's a free faith. You may choose the crooked way. He will not keep you against your will. But it is not the kind of thing you fall into by chance or slip into by ignorance. Defection requires a deliberate sustained and determined act of rejection.

All the persons of faith I know are sinners, doubters, uneven performers. We are secure not because we are sure of ourselves but because we trust that God is sure of us. The opening phrase of the psalm is "those who trust in the LORD"—not those who trust in their performance, in their morals, in their righteousness, in their health, in their pastor, in their doctor, in their president, in their economy, in their nation—"those who trust in the LORD." Those who decide that God is for us and will make us whole eternally.

Mountain Climbers Roped Together

When I was a child I walked about a mile to school each day with my two best friends. Along a quarter of that distance there was a railway track. When we came to that stretch we always walked on the rails. Each of us wanted to make it all the way without falling off, but didn't want the others to similarly succeed. We would throw things at each other to upset balance, or say things to divert attention, cry out that the train was coming, or announce that there was a dead body in the ditch. There are some who have supposed that that is what Christian living is, teetering and wobbling along that rail, taunted by the devil and his angels. With some skill and a lot of luck we might just make it to heaven, but it's an uncertain business at best.

Psalm 125 says that is not the way it is at all. Being a Christian is like sitting in the middle of Jerusalem, fortified and secure. "First we are established and then entrenched; settled, and then sentinalled: made like a mount, and then protected as if by mountains."[5] And so the last sentence is, "Peace be in Israel!" A colloquial, but in the context accurate, translation would be, "Relax." We are secure. God is running the show. Neither our feelings of depression nor the facts of suffering nor the possibilities of defection are evidence that God has abandoned us. There is nothing more certain than that he will accomplish his salvation in our lives and perfect his will in our histories. Three times in his great Sermon, Jesus, knowing how easily we imagine the worst, repeats the reassuring command, "Do not be anxious. . . . " (Mt. 6:25, 31, 34). Our life with God is a sure thing.

When mountain climbers are in dangerous terrain, on the face of a cliff or on the slopes of a glacier, they rope themselves together. Sometimes one of them slips and falls—backslides. But not everyone falls at once, and so those who are still on their feet are able to keep the backslider from falling away completely. And of course, in any group of climbers, there is a veteran and experienced climber in the lead, identified for us in the letter to the Hebrews as "Jesus, who leads us in our faith and brings it to perfection" (Heb. 12:2 JB).

Traveling in the way of faith and climbing the ascent to Christ may be difficult, but it is not worrisome. The weather may be adverse but it is never fatal. We may slip and stumble and fall, but the rope will hold us.

8: Joy

"Our Mouth Was Filled with Laughter"

When the LORD restored the fortunes
*   of Zion,*
*   we were like those who dream.*
Then our mouth was filled with laughter,
*   and our tongue with shouts of joy;*
then they said among the nations,
*   "The LORD has done great things for them."*
The LORD has done great things for us;
*   we are glad.*

Restore our fortunes, O LORD,
*   like the watercourses in the Negeb!*
May those who sow in tears
*   reap with shouts of joy!*
He that goes forth weeping,
*   bearing the seed for sowing,*
shall come home with shouts of joy,
*   bringing his sheaves with him.*

Psalm 126

**I have read that during the process of
canonization the Catholic Church
demands proof of joy in the candidate,**

and although I have not been able to
track down chapter and verse I like
the suggestion that dourness is not a
sacred attribute.

Phyllis McGinley

Ellen Glasgow, in her autobiography, tells of her father who was a Presbyterian elder, full of rectitude and rigid with duty: "He was entirely unselfish, and in his long life he never committed a pleasure."[1] Peter Jay, in a recent political column in the *Baltimore Sun*, described the sober intensity and the personal austerities of one of our Maryland politicians, and then threw in this line: "He dresses like a Presbyterian."

I know there are Christians, so-called, who never crack a smile and who can't abide a joke, and I suppose Presbyterians contribute their quota. But I don't meet very many of them. The stereotype as such is a big lie created, presumably, by the devil. One of the delightful discoveries along the way of Christian discipleship is how much enjoyment there is, how much laughter you hear, how much sheer fun you find.

In Phyllis McGinley's delightful book *Saint-Watching* there is this story: "Martin Luther's close friend was Philipp Melanchthon, author of the Augsburg Confession. Melanchthon was a cool man where Luther was fervid, a scholar opposed to a doer, and he continued to live like a monk even after he had joined the German reformation. . . . One day Luther lost patience with Melanchthon's virtuous reserve. 'For heaven's sake,' he roared, 'why don't you go out and sin a little? God deserves to have something to forgive you for!' "[2]

A Consequence Not a Requirement

"Our mouth was filled with laughter, and our tongue with shouts of joy." That is the authentic Christian note, a sign of those who are on the way of salvation. Joy is characteristic of Christian pilgrimage. It is the second in Paul's list of the

fruits of the Spirit (Gal. 5:22). It is the first of Jesus' signs
in the Gospel of John (turning water into wine). It was said
of the Hasid, Levi-Yitzhak of Berditchev: "His smiles were
fraught with greater meaning than his sermons."[3] The
same thing can be said of much of the Bible: its smiles
carry more meaning than its sermons.

This is not to say that joy is a moral requirement for
Christian living. Some of us experience things that are full
of sadness and pain. Some of us descend to low points in
our lives when joy seems to have permanently departed.
We must not in such circumstances or during such times
say, "Well, that's the final proof that I am not a good Christian. Christians are supposed to have their mouths filled
with laughter and tongues with shouts of joy; and I don't.
I'm not joyful, therefore I must not be a Christian."

Joy is not a requirement of Christian discipleship, it is a
consequence. It is not what we have to acquire in order to
experience life in Christ; it is what comes to us when we are
walking in the way of faith and obedience.

We come to God (and to the revelation of God's ways)
because none of us have it within ourselves, except momen-
tarily, to be joyous. Joy is a product of abundance; it is the
overflow of vitality. It is life working together harmoniously. It is exuberance. Inadequate sinners as we are, none of
us can manage that for very long.

We try to get it through entertainment. We pay someone
to make jokes, tell stories, perform dramatic actions, sing
songs. We buy the vitality of another's imagination to divert
and enliven our own poor lives. The enormous entertainment industry in our land is a sign of the depletion of joy
in our culture. Society is a bored, gluttonous king employing a court jester to divert it after an overindulgent meal.
But that kind of joy never penetrates our lives, never
changes our basic constitution. The effects are extremely
temporary—a few minutes, a few hours, a few days at most.

When we run out of money, the joy trickles away. We cannot make ourselves joyful. Joy cannot be commanded, purchased or arranged.

But there is something we can do. We can decide to live in response to the abundance of God, and not under the dictatorship of our own poor needs. We can decide to live in the environment of a living God and not our own dying selves. We can decide to center ourselves in the God who generously gives and not in our own egos which greedily grab. One of the certain consequences of such a life is joy, the kind expressed in Psalm 126.

Joy: Past, Present, Future

The center sentence in the psalm is, "We are glad" (v. 3). The words on one side of that center (vv. 1-2) are in the past tense, the words on the other side (vv. 4-6) in the future tense. Present gladness has past and future. It is not an ephemeral emotion. It is not a spurt of good feelings that comes when the weather and the stock market are both right on the same day.

The background for joy is only alluded to here, but the words trigger vast memories: "When the LORD restored the fortunes of Zion . . . then our mouth was filled with laughter, and our tongue with shouts of joy; then they said among the nations, 'The LORD has done great things for them.' The LORD has done great things for us; we are glad."

What were the "great things"? On nearly any page of the Bible we find them. There is the story of God's people in a long, apparently interminable servitude under the shadows of the Egyptian pyramids and the lash of harsh masters. And then, suddenly and without warning, it was over. One day they were making "bricks without straw" and the next they were running up the far slopes of the Red Sea, shouting the great song, "I will sing to the LORD, for he has triumphed gloriously; the horse and his rider he has thrown into the sea. The LORD is my strength and my song, and he has become my salvation; this is my God, and I will praise him, my father's God, and I will exalt him" (Ex. 15: 1-2).

We turn over a few pages and find the story of David. There were years of wilderness guerrilla warfare against the Philistines, a perilous existence with moody, manic King Saul, a painful groping through the guilt of murder and adultery, then in his old age chased from his throne by his own son and forced to set up a government in exile. And, at the end, his song. It begins with gratitude: "The LORD is my rock, and my fortress, and my deliverer"; it ends in confidence, "The Lord lives; and blessed be my rock." In the center there is a rocket burst of joy: "Yea, by thee I can crush a troop, and by my God I can leap over a wall" (2 Sam. 22: 2, 47, 30).

We turn a few more pages and find the terrible story of Babylonian captivity. Israel experienced the worst that can come to any of us: rape in the streets, cannibalism in the kitchens, neighbors reduced to bestiality, a six-hundred-mile forced march across a desert, the taunting mockeries by the captors. And then, incredibly—joy. Beginning with the low, gentle words, "Comfort, comfort my people, says your God. Speak tenderly to Jerusalem, and cry to her that her warfare is ended, that her iniquity is pardoned" (Is. 40:1-2). And then the swelling reassurances of help: "When you pass through the waters I will be with you. . . .Fear not" (43:2-5). The sounds combine and surge to a proclamation: "How beautiful upon the mountains are the feet of him who brings good tidings. . . . Hark, your watchmen lift up their voice, together they sing for joy" (52:7-8). The gratitude and gladness builds and soars. There is a sea-change into joy.

"When the LORD restored the fortunes of Zion, we were like those who dream." Each act of God was an impossible miracle. There was no way it could have happened, and it did happen. "We were like those who dream." We nurture these memories of laughter, these shouts of joy. We fill our minds with the stories of God's acts. Joy has a history. Joy is the verified, repeated experience of those involved in what God is doing. It is as real as a date in history, as solid as a stratum of rock in Palestine. Joy is nurtured by living in such a history, building on such a foundation.

Joyful Expectation

The other side of "we are glad" (vv. 4-6) is in the future tense. Joy is nurtured by anticipation. If the joy-producing acts of God are characteristic of our past as God's people, they will also be characteristic of our future as his people. There is no reason to suppose that God will arbitrarily change his way of working with us. What we have known of him, we will know of him. Just as joy builds on the past, it borrows from the future. It expects certain things to happen.

Two images fix the hope: The first is "Restore our fortunes, O LORD, like the watercourses in the Negeb!" The Negeb, the south of Israel, is a vast desert. The watercourses of the Negeb are a network of ditches cut into the soil by wind and rain erosion. For most of the year they are baked dry under the sun, but a sudden rain makes the desert ablaze with blossoms. With such suddenness long years of barren waiting are interrupted by God's invasion of grace into our lives.

The second image is "May those who sow in tears reap with shouts of joy! He that goes forth weeping, bearing the seed for sowing, shall come home with shouts of joy, bringing his sheaves with him." The hard work of sowing seed in what looks like perfectly empty earth has, as every farmer knows, a time of harvest. All suffering, all pain, all emptiness, all disappointment is seed: sow it in God, he will, finally, bring a crop of joy from it.

It is clear in Psalm 126 that the one who wrote it and those who sang it were no strangers to the dark side of things. They carried the painful memory of exile in their bones and the scars of oppression on their backs. They knew the deserts of the heart and the nights of weeping. They knew what it meant to sow in tears.

One of the most interesting and remarkable things that Christians learn is that laughter does not exclude weeping. Christian joy is not an escape from sorrow. Pain and hardship still come, but they are unable to drive out the happiness of the redeemed.

A common but futile strategy for achieving joy is trying to eliminate things that hurt: get rid of pain by numbing the nerve ends, get rid of insecurity by eliminating risks, get rid of disappointments by depersonalizing your relationships. And then try to lighten the boredom of such a life by buying joy in the form of vacations and entertainment. There isn't a hint of that in Psalm 126.

Laughter is a result of living in the midst of God's great works ("when the Lord restored . . . our mouth was filled with laughter"). Enjoyment is not an escape from boredom but a plunge by faith into God's work ("he that goes forth weeping, bearing the seed for sowing, shall come home with shouts of joy, bringing his sheaves with him"). There is plenty of suffering on both sides, past and future. The joy comes because God knows how to wipe away tears, and, in his resurrection work, create the smile of new life. Joy is what God gives, not what we work up. Laughter is the delight that things are working together for good to them that love God, not the giggles that betray the nervousness of a precarious defense system. The joy that develops in the Christian way of discipleship is an overflow of spirits that comes from feeling good not about yourself but about God. We find that his ways are dependable, his promises sure.

This joy is not dependent on our good luck in escaping hardship. It is not dependent on our good health and avoiding pain. Christian joy is actual in the midst of pain, suffering, loneliness and misfortune. St. Paul is our most convincing witness to this. One of his great, characteristic words is *rejoice*. The word is tympanic, resonating through every movement of his life: "We rejoice in our sufferings, knowing that suffering produces endurance, and endurance produces character, and character produces hope, and hope does not disappoint us, because God's love has been . . . given to us. . . . We also rejoice in God through our Lord Jesus Christ, through whom we have now received our reconciliation" (Rom. 5:3-5, 11). That is the fulfillment of the prayer, "Restore our fortunes, O LORD, like the watercourses in the Negeb!"

And then out of his prison cell we hear Paul's trumpeting conclusion to his Philippian letter: "Rejoice in the Lord always; again I will say, Rejoice. Let all men know your forbearance. The Lord is at hand" (Phil. 4:4-5). There is no grim, Greek Stoicism in that; it is a robust, Welsh hymn, striding from sorrow into song. It is the end result of the petition: "May those who sow in tears reap with shouts of joy!" The witness is repeated over and over again, through the generations and has scattered representatives through every community of Christians.

The psalm does not give us this joy as a package or as a formula, but there are some things it does do. It shows up the tinniness of the world's joy and affirms the solidity of God's joy. It reminds us of the accelerating costs and diminishing returns of those who pursue pleasure as a path toward joy. It introduces us to the way of discipleship which has consequences in joy. It encourages us in the way of faith to both experience and share joy. It tells the story of God's acts which put laughter into people's mouths and shouts on their tongues. It repeats the promises of a God who accom-

panies his wandering, weeping children until they arrive
home, exuberant, "bringing in the sheaves." It announces
the existence of a people who assemble to worship God and
disperse to live to God's glory, whose lives are bordered on
one side by a memory of God's acts and the other by hope
in God's promises, and who along with whatever else is hap-
pening are able to say, at the center, "We are glad."

9: Work

"Unless the LORD Builds the House"

Unless the LORD builds the house,
  those who build it labor in vain.
Unless the LORD watches over the city,
  the watchman stays awake in vain.
It is in vain that you rise up early and go late
  to rest,
eating the bread of anxious toil;
  for he gives to his beloved sleep.

Lo, sons are a heritage from the LORD,
  the fruit of the womb a reward.
Like arrows in the hand of a warrior
  are the sons of one's youth.
Happy is the man who has
  his quiver full of them!
He shall not be put to shame
  when he speaks with his enemies in the gate.

Psalm 127

**The first great fact which emerges from
our civilization is that today everything
has become "means." There is no
longer an "end"; we do not know whither
we are going. We have forgotten our**

collective ends, and we possess great
means: we set huge machines in
motion in order to arrive nowhere.

Jacques Ellul

The greatest work project of the ancient world is a story of disaster. The unexcelled organization and enormous energy that were concentrated in building the Tower of Babel resulted in such a shattered community and garbled communication that civilization is still trying to recover. Effort, even if the effort is religious (perhaps *especially* when the effort is religious), does not in itself justify anything.

One of the tasks of Christian discipleship is to learn how to "do the works you did at first" (Rev. 2:5) and absolutely refuse to "work like the devil." Work is a major component in most lives. It is unavoidable. It can be either good or bad, an area where our sin is magnified or where our faith matures. For it is the nature of sin to take good things and twist them, ever so slightly, so that they miss the target to which they were aimed, the target of God. One requirement of discipleship is to learn the ways in which sin skews our nature and submit what we learn to the continuing will of God so that we are reshaped through the days of our obedience.

Psalm 127 shows both the right way and the wrong way to work. It posts a warning and provides the example which guide Christians in work that is done to the glory of God.

Babel or Buddhist

Psalm 127 first posts a warning about work: "Unless the LORD builds the house, those who build it labor in vain. Unless the LORD watches over the city, the watchman stays awake in vain. It is in vain that you rise up early and go late to rest, eating the bread of anxious toil; for he gives to his beloved sleep."

Some people have read these verses and paraphrased

them to read like this: "You don't have to work hard to be
a Christian. You don't have to put yourself out at all. Go to
sleep. God is doing everything that needs to be done." St.
Paul had to deal with some of these people in the church at
Thessalonica. They were saying that since God had done
everything in Christ there was nothing more for them to
do. If all effort ends up in godless confusion (as it did with
the people at Babel) or in hypocritic self-righteousness (as
had happened among the Pharisees), the obvious and
Christian solution is to quit work and wait for the Lord to
come. With a magnificent redeemer like our Lord Jesus
Christ and a majestic God like our Father in heaven, what
is there left to do? And so they sat around, doing nothing.

Meanwhile they lived "by faith" off their less spiritual
friends. Unfriendly critics might have called them free-
loaders. Paul became angry and told them to get to work:
"We hear that some of you are living in idleness, mere
busybodies, not doing any work. Now such persons we command and exhort in the Lord Jesus Christ to do their work
in quietness and to earn their own living. Brethren, do not
be weary in well-doing" (2 Thess. 3:11-13). How did they
dare to reinterpret the gospel into a rationalization for
sloth when he, Paul, from whom they had learned the
gospel "worked night and day, that we might not burden
any of you" (1 Thess. 2:9).

The Christian has to find a better way to avoid the
sin of Babel than by imitating the lilies of the field, who
"neither toil nor spin." The pretentious work which became
Babel and its pious opposite which developed at Thessalonica are displayed today on the broad canvasses of
Western and Eastern cultures respectively.

Western culture takes up where Babel left off and deifies
human effort as such. The machine is the symbol of this
way of life that attempts to control and manage. Technology promises to give us control over the earth and over

other people. But the promise is not fulfilled: lethal auto-mobiles, ugly buildings and ponderous bureaucracies ravage the earth and empty lives of meaning. Structures become more important than the people who live in them. Machines become more important than the people who use them. We care more for our possessions with which we hope to make our way in the world than with our thoughts and dreams which tell us who we are in the world.

Eastern culture, on the other hand, is a variation on the Thessalonican view. There is a deep-rooted pessimism regarding human effort. Since all work is tainted with selfishness and pride, the solution is to withdraw from all activity into pure being. The symbol of such an attitude is the Buddha—an enormous fat person sitting cross-legged, looking at his own navel. Motionless, inert, quiet. All trouble comes from doing too much; therefore, do noth-ing. Step out of the rat race. The world of motion is evil, so quit doing everything. Say as little as possible; do as little as possible; finally, at the point of perfection, you will say nothing and do nothing. The goal is to withdraw absolutely and finally from action, from thought, from passion.

The two cultures are in collision today and many think that we must choose between them. But there is another option: Psalm 127 shows a way to work which is neither sheer activity nor pure passivity. It doesn't glorify work as such and it doesn't condemn work as such. It doesn't say, "God has a great work for you to do; go and do it." Nor does it say, "God has done everything; go fishing." If we want simple solutions in regard to work we can be-come workaholics or dropouts. If we want to experience the fullness of work, we will do better to study Psalm 127.

In the Beginning God Worked
The premise of the psalm for all work is that God works:

"Unless the LORD builds the house. ... Unless the LORD watches over the city. ... " The condition *unless* presupposes that God does work: he builds; he watches.

The main difference between Christians and others is that we take God seriously and they do not. We really do believe that he is the central reality of all existence. We really do pay attention to what he is and to what he does. We really do order our lives in response to that reality and not to some other. Paying attention to God involves a realization that he works.

The Bible begins with the announcement, "In the beginning God created ... " not "sat majestic in the heavens," and not "was filled with beauty and love." He created. He *did* something. He *made* something. He fashioned heaven and earth. The week of creation was a week of work. The days are described not by their weather conditions and not by their horoscope readings: Genesis 1 is a journal of work. We live in a universe and in a history where God is working. Before anything else, work is an activity of God. Before we go to the sociologists for a description of work or to the psychologists for insight into work or to the economists for an analysis of work, we must comprehend the biblical record: God works. The work of God is defined and described in the pages of Scripture. We have models of creation, acts of redemption, examples of help and compassion, paradigms of comfort and salvation. One of the reasons that Christians read Scripture repeatedly and carefully is to find out just how God works in Jesus Christ so that we can work in the name of Jesus Christ.

In every letter St. Paul wrote he demonstrated that a Christian's work is a natural, inevitable and faithful development out of God's work. Each of his letters concludes with a series of directives which guide us into the kind of work that participates in God's work. The curse of some people's lives is not work, as such, but senseless work, vain

The entire miracle of procreation and reproduction requires our participation, but hardly in the form of what we call our work. We did not make these marvelous creatures that walk and talk and grow among us. We participated in an act of love which was provided for us in the structure of God's creation.

Jesus leads us to understand the psalmist's "sons" in terms representative of all intimate and personal relationships. He himself did not procreate children, yet by his love he made us all sons and daughters (Mt. 12:46-50). His job description was "My Father is working still, and I am working" (Jn. 5:17). By joining Jesus and the psalm we learn a way of work which does not acquire things or amass possessions but responds to God and develops relationships. People are at the center of Christian work. In the way of pilgrimage we do not drive cumbersome Conestoga wagons loaded down with baggage over endless prairies. We travel light. The character of our work is shaped not by accomplishments or possessions but in the birth of relationships: "Sons are a heritage from the LORD." We invest our energy in people. Among those around us we develop sons and daughters, sisters and brothers even as our Lord did with us: "Happy is the man who has his quiver full of them!"

For it makes very little difference how much money Christians carry in their wallets or purses. It makes little difference how our culture values and rewards our work . . . *unless*. For our work creates neither life nor righteousness. Relentless, compulsive work habits ("the bread of anxious toil") which our society rewards and admires are seen by the psalmist as a sign of weak faith and assertive pride, as if God could not be trusted to accomplish his will, as if we could rearrange the universe by our own effort.

What does make a difference is the personal relation-

The entire miracle of procreation and reproduction requires our participation, but hardly in the form of what we call our work. We did not make these marvelous creatures that walk and talk and grow among us. We participated in an act of love which was provided for us in the structure of God's creation.

Jesus leads us to understand the psalmist's "sons" in terms representative of all intimate and personal relationships. He himself did not procreate children, yet by his love he made us all sons and daughters (Mt. 12:46-50). His job description was "My Father is working still, and I am working" (Jn. 5:17). By joining Jesus and the psalm we learn a way of work which does not acquire things or amass possessions but responds to God and develops relationships. People are at the center of Christian work. In the way of pilgrimage we do not drive cumbersome Conestoga wagons loaded down with baggage over endless prairies. We travel light. The character of our work is shaped not by accomplishments or possessions but in the birth of relationships: "Sons are a heritage from the LORD." We invest our energy in people. Among those around us we develop sons and daughters, sisters and brothers even as our Lord did with us: "Happy is the man who has his quiver full of them!"

For it makes very little difference how much money Christians carry in their wallets or purses. It makes little difference how our culture values and rewards our work . . . *unless.* For our work creates neither life nor righteousness. Relentless, compulsive work habits ("the bread of anxious toil") which our society rewards and admires are seen by the psalmist as a sign of weak faith and assertive pride, as if God could not be trusted to accomplish his will, as if we could rearrange the universe by our own effort.

What does make a difference is the personal relation-

work, futile work, work that takes place apart from God, work that ignores the *unless*. Christian discipleship, by orienting us in God's work and setting us in the mainstream of what God is already doing, frees us from the compulsiveness of work. Hilary of Tours taught that every Christian had to be constantly vigilant against what he called *"Irreligiosa solicitudo pro Deo"*—a blasphemous anxiety to do God's work for him.[1]

Our work goes wrong when we lose touch with the God who works "his salvation in the midst of the earth." It goes wrong both when we work anxiously and when we don't work at all, when we become frantic and compulsive in our work (Babel) and when we become indolent and lethargic in our work (Thessalonica). The foundational truth is that work is good. If God does it, it must be all right. Work has dignity: there can be nothing degrading about work if God works. Work has purpose: there can be nothing futile about work if God works.

Effortless Work

The psalm not only posts a warning, it gives an example: "Lo, sons are a heritage from the LORD, the fruit of the womb a reward. Like arrows in the hand of a warrior are the sons of one's youth. Happy is the man who has his quiver full of them! He shall not be put to shame when he speaks with his enemies in the gate."

In contrast to the anxious labor that builds cities and guards possessions, the psalm praises the effortless work of making children. Opposed to the strenuous efforts of persons who, in doubt of God's providence and mistrust of man's love, seek their own gain by godless struggles is the gift of children, born not through human effort, but through the miraculous processes of reproduction which God has created among us. The example couldn't have been better chosen. What do we do to get sons? Very little.

ships that we create and develop. We learn a name; we start a friendship; we follow up on a smile—or maybe even on a grimace. Nature is profligate with its seeds, scattering them everywhere; a few of them sprout. Out of numerous handshakes and greetings, some germinate and grow into a friendship in Christ. Christian worship gathers the energy and focuses the motivation which transform us from consumers who use work to get things into people who are intimate and in whom work is a way of being in creative relationship with another. Such work can be done within the structure of any job, career or profession. As Christians do the jobs and tasks assigned to them in what the world calls work, we learn to pay attention to and practice what God is doing in love and justice, in helping and healing, in liberating and cheering.

The first people to sing this psalm had expended much effort to get to Jerusalem. Some came great distances and overcame formidable difficulties. Would there be a tendency among the pilgrims to congratulate one another on their successful journeys, to swell with pride in their accomplishment, to trade stories of their experiences? Would there be comparisons on who made the longest pilgrimage, the fastest pilgrimage, who had brought the most neighbors, who had come the most times? Then, through the noise of the crowd someone would strike up the tune, "Unless the LORD. . . . " The pilgrimage is not at the center; the Lord is at the center. No matter how hard they struggled to get there, no matter what they did in the way of heroics—fending off bandits, clubbing lions and crushing wolves—that is not what is to be sung. Psalm 127 insists on a perspective in which our effort is at the periphery and God's work is at the center.

10: Happiness

"You Shall Be Happy, and It Shall Be Well with You"

Blessed is every one who fears the LORD,
*   who walks in his ways!*
You shall eat the fruit of the labor of your hands;
*   you shall be happy, and it shall be well*
*   with you.*

Your wife will be like a fruitful vine
*   within your house;*
your children will be like olive shoots
*   around your table.*
Lo, thus shall the man be blessed
*   who fears the LORD.*

The LORD bless you from Zion!
*   May you see the prosperity of Jerusalem*
*   all the days of your life!*
May you see your children's children!
*   Peace be upon Israel!*

Psalm 128

Joy, which was the small publicity of the pagan, is the gigantic secret of the Christian.

G. K. Chesterton

There is a general assumption prevalent in the world that it is extremely difficult to be a Christian. While it is true that many don't completely disqualify themselves, they do modify their claims: *ordinary* Christians they call themselves. They respect the church, worship fairly regularly, try to live decently. But they also give themselves somewhat generous margins to allow for the temptations and pressures put upon them by the world. To *really* be on the way of faith, take with absolute *seriousness* all that the Bible says—well, that requires a predisposition to saintliness, extraordinary will power and an unspecified number of nameless austerities that they are quite sure they cannot manage.

But this is as far from the truth as the east is from the west. The easiest thing in the world is to be a Christian. What is hard is to be a sinner. Being a Christian is what we were created for. The life of faith has the support of an entire creation and the resources of a magnificent redemption. The structure of this world was created by God so we could live in it easily and happily as his children. The history we walk in has been repeatedly entered by God, most notably in Jesus Christ, first to show us and then to help us live full of faith and exuberant with purpose. In the course of Christian discipleship we discover that without Christ we were doing it the hard way and that with Christ we are doing it the easy way. It is not Christians who have it hard, but non-Christians.

Promises and Pronouncements
Blessing is the word that describes this happy state of affairs. Psalm 128 features the word. The psalm begins with three descriptive promises: "Blessed is every one who fears

the LORD, who walks in his ways!" "You shall eat the fruit of the labor of your hands." "You shall be happy [Hebrew, *blessed*], and it shall be well with you." It concludes with three vigorous pronouncements: "The LORD bless you from Zion!" "May you see the prosperity of Jerusalem all the days of your life!" "May you see your children's children!" Sandwiched between those promises and pronouncements is an illustration of blessing: "Your wife will be like a fruitful vine within your house; your children will be like olive shoots around your table. Lo, thus shall the man be blessed who fears the LORD."[1]

That all adds up to a good life—a life that is bound on one side by promises of blessing, on the other side by pronouncements of blessing and which experiences blessings between those boundaries.

The Bible is one long exposition of this blessing. In Genesis, God, having completed the work of creation by making man male and female, "blessed them" (Gen. 1:28). He called Abraham and promised, "I will make of you a great nation, and I will bless you, and make your name great, so that you will be a blessing" (Gen. 12:2). Each of the twelve tribes of Israel receives a special blessing which identifies its particular characteristic of vitality (Gen. 49). David, who in so many ways embodied the intensities and joys of faith was "richer in blessing than any other Israelite" —a long series of blessings, not without sorrow to be sure, but always brimming with life. Jesus, in his introduction to his Sermon on the Mount, identifies the eight key qualities in the life of a person of faith and announces each one with the word *blessed.* He makes it clear that the way of discipleship is not a reduction in what we already are, not an attenuation of our lives, not a subtraction from what we are used to. He will rather expand our capacities and fill us up with life so that we overflow with joy. The conclusion of the Bible is that great, thunderous book of

Revelation in which there are seven salvos of blessing (1:3; 14:13; 16:15; 19:9; 20:6; 22:7, 14). The blessings cannonade back and forth across the battlefield on which Christ completes his victory over sin and establishes his eternal rule. "The whole book stands in the framework of the blessing of those who attain to and keep the blessed revelation of the mysteries of God (1:3 confirmed in 22:7)."[2]

As we read this story of blessing and familiarize ourselves with the men and women who are experiencing God's blessing, we realize that it is not something external or ephemeral. Not a matter of having a good day, not an occasional run of luck. It is an "inner strength of the soul and the happiness it creates, . . . the vital power, without which no living being can exist. Happiness cannot be given to a person as something lying outside him. . . . The action of God does not fall outside but at the very center of the soul; that which it gives us is not something external, but the energy, the power of creating it. . . . The blessing thus comprises the power to live in its deepest and most comprehensive sense. Nothing which belongs to action and to making life real can fall outside the blessing. . . . Blessing is the vital power, without which no living being can exist."[3]

It is this that fills and surrounds the person who is on the way of faith.

Sharing in Life

The illustration that forms the center of the psalm shows how the blessing works: "Your wife will be like a fruitful vine within your house; your children will be like olive shoots around your table." The illustration is, as we would expect, conditioned by Hebrew culture in which the standard signs of happiness were a wife who had many children and children who gathered and grew around the table: fruitful vine and olive shoots. This illustration is just that, an example which we need not reproduce exactly in order to experience blessing. (We, for instance, don't try to have as many children as possible—and try to get them to stay at home for all their lives!) But the meaning is still with us: blessing has inherent in it the power to increase. It functions by the sharing and delight in life. "Life consists in the constant meeting of souls, which must share their contents with each other. The blessed gives to the others, because the strength instinctively pours from him and up around him. . . . The characteristic of blessing is to multiply."[4]

John Calvin, preaching to his congregation in Geneva, Switzerland, pointed out to his parishioners that we must develop better and deeper concepts of happiness from those held by the world which makes a happy life to consist in "ease, honours, and great wealth."[5] Psalm 128 helps us do that. Too much of the world's happiness depends on taking from one to satisfy another. To increase my standard of living, someone in another part of the world must lower his. The worldwide crisis of hunger that we face today is a result of that method of pursuing happiness. Industrialized nations acquire appetites for more and more luxuries and higher and higher standards of living, and increasing numbers of people are made poor and hungry. It doesn't have to be that way. The experts on the world hunger problem say that there is enough to go around right now. We don't have a production problem. We have the agricultural capability to produce enough food. We have the transportation technology to distribute the food. But we have a greed problem: if I don't grab mine while I can, I might not be happy. The hunger problem is not going to be solved by government or by industry, but in church, among Christians who learn a different way to pursue happiness.

Christian blessing is a realizing that "it is more blessed to give than to receive." As we learn to give and to share, our vitality increases and the people around us become "fruitful vines" and "olive shoots" around our tables.

The blessings that are promised to, pronounced upon and experienced by Christians, do not of course exclude difficulties. The Bible never indicates that. But the difficulties are not inherent in the faith: they come from the outside in the form of temptations, seductions, pressures. Not a day goes by but what we have to deal with that ancient triple threat that Christians in the Middle Ages summarized under the headings of the world, the flesh, and the devil: the world—the society of proud and arrogant mankind that defies and tries to eliminate God's rule and presence in history; the flesh—the corruption that sin has introduced into our very appetites and instincts; and the devil—the malignant will that tempts and seduces us away from the will of God. We have to contend with all of that. We are in a battle. There is a fight of faith to be waged. But the way of faith itself is in tune with what God has done and is doing. The road we travel is the well-traveled road of discipleship. It is not a way of boredom or despair or confusion. It is not a miserable groping, but a way of blessing.

Traveling by the Roads
There are no tricks involved in getting in on this life of blessing, and no luck required. We simply become Christians and begin the life of faith. We acknowledge God as our maker and lover, and accept Christ as the means by which we can be in living relationship with God. We accept the announced and proclaimed truth that God is at the center of our existence, find out how he has constructed this world (his creation), how he has provided for our redemption, and proceed to walk in that way. In the plain words of the psalm: "Blessed is every one who fears the LORD, who walks in his ways!"

"Fears the LORD." *Reverence* might be a better word. Awe. The Bible isn't interested in whether we believe in God or not. It assumes that everyone more or less does. What it is interested in is the response we have toward him: will we let God be as he is, majestic and holy, vast and wondrous, or will we always be trying to whittle him down to the size of our small minds, insist on confining him within the boundaries we are comfortable with, refuse to think of him other than in images that are convenient to our lifestyle? But then we are not dealing with the God of creation and the Christ of the cross, but with a dime-store reproduction of something made in our image, usually for commercial reasons. To guard against all such blasphemous chumminess with the Almighty, the Bible talks of the fear of the LORD—not to scare us but to bring us to awesome attention before the overwhelming grandeur of God, to shut up our whining and chattering and stop our running and fidgeting so that we can really see him as he is and listen to him as he speaks his merciful, life-changing words of forgiveness.

"Walk in his ways." We not only let God be God as he really is, but we start doing the things for which he made us. We take a certain route; we follow certain directions; we do specified things. There are ethical standards to follow, there are moral values to foster, there are spiritual disciplines to practice, there is social justice to pursue, there are personal relationships to develop. None of it is difficult to understand. "Mere ethics," quipped Austin Farrer once, "call for no such august or mysterious explanation; next to plumbing, morality is social convenience number one. . . . "6

Because of the ambiguities of the world we live in and the defects in our own wills, we will not do any of this perfectly and without fault. But that isn't the point. The way is plain—walk in it. Keeping the rules and obeying the commands is only common sense. People who are forever breaking the rules, trying other roads, attempting to create their own system of values and truth from scratch, spend most of their time calling up someone to get them out of trouble and help repair the damages, and then ask the silly question, "What went wrong?" As H. H. Farmer said, "If you go against the grain of the universe you get splinters."

Some who read Psalm 128 will say, "Of course, that's the way it is with me. Doesn't everyone feel that?" and others will only be puzzled by how anyone could sing such a cheerful song in such a messed-up world. John Henry Newman once explained it this way: "If I want to travel north and all the roads are cut to the east, of course I shall complain of the roads. I shall find nothing but obstacles; I shall have to surmount walls, and cross rivers, and go round about, and after all fail of my end." Such is the conduct of those who are trying to achieve some meaning in their lives, pursuing their right to happiness, but refusing to take the well-traveled roads that lead there. They are trying to get to Mount Zion but ignore all the signposts and compass readings, and stubbornly avoid the trails as they bushwack their way through wilderness. "Do you not see that they necessarily must meet with thwartings, crossings, disappointments, and failure?" They go mile after mile, watching in vain for their destination, but never sighting it. "And then they accuse religion of interfering with what they consider their innocent pleasures and wishes." But religion is only an inconvenience to those who are traveling against the grain of creation, at cross-purposes with the way which leads to redemption.[7]

Everyone wants to be happy, to be blessed. Too many people are willfully refusing to pay attention to the one who wills our happiness and ignorantly supposing that the Christian way is a harder way to get what they want than

doing it on their own. But they are wrong. God's ways and
God's presence are where we experience the happiness that
lasts. Do it the easy way: "Blessed is every one who fears
the LORD, who walks in his ways!"

11: Perseverance

"Yet They Have Not Prevailed against Me"

"Sorely have they afflicted me from my youth,"
  let Israel now say—
"Sorely have they afflicted me from my youth,
  yet they have not prevailed against me.
The plowers plowed upon my back;
  they made long their furrows."
The LORD is righteous;
  he has cut the cords of the wicked.
May all who hate Zion
  be put to shame and turned backward!
Let them be like the grass on the housetops,
  which withers before it grows up,
with which the reaper does not fill his hand
  or the binder of sheaves his bosom,
while those who pass by do not say,
  "The blessing of the LORD be upon you!
We bless you in the name of the LORD!"

Psalm 129

Patience is drawing on underlying forces; it is powerfully positive, though to a natural view it looks like just sitting it out. How would I persist against positive eroding forces if I were not

drawing on invisible forces? And
patience has a positive tonic effect on
others; because of the presence of
the patient person, they revive and go on,
as if he were the gyroscope of the ship
providing a stable ground. But the
patient person himself does not enjoy it.

Paul Goodman

S tick-to-it-iveness is one of the more inelegant words in the language, but I have a special fondness for it nevertheless. I heard the word a great deal when I was young, mostly, as I recall, from my mother. I was a creature of sudden but short-lived enthusiasms. I had a passion for building model airplanes, and then one day, mysteriously, all desire left and the basement was littered with half-finished models. Then stamp-collecting became an all-consuming hobby. I received an immense stamp album for Christmas, joined a philatelic club, acquired piles and piles of stamps and then one day, unaccountably, the interest left me. The album gathered dust and the mounds of stamps were left unmounted. Next it was horses. Each Saturday morning my best friend and I would ride our bikes to a dude ranch two miles from town, get horses and ride up into the Montana foothills imagining we were Merriweather Lewis and William Clark, or, less pretentiously, Gene Autry and the Lone Ranger. And then, overnight, that entire world vanished and in its place was —girls.

It was during these rather frequent transitions from one enthusiasm to another that I was slapped with the reprimand, "Eugene, you have no stick-to-it-iveness. You never finish anything." Years later I learned that the church had a fancier word for the same thing: *perseverance.* I have also found that it is one of the marks of Christian discipleship and have learned to admire those who exemplified it. Along the way Psalm 129 has gotten included in my admiration.

Tough Faith

" 'Sorely have they afflicted me from my youth,' let Israel

now say—'Sorely have they afflicted me from my youth, yet they have not prevailed against me.' " The people of God are tough. For long centuries those who belong to the world have waged war against the way of faith, and they have yet to win. They have tried everything, but none of it has worked. They have tried persecution and ridicule, torture and exile, but the way of faith has continued healthy and robust: "Sorely have they afflicted me from my youth, yet they have not prevailed against me."

Do you think of Christian faith as a fragile style of life that can flourish only when the weather conditions are just right, or do you see it as a tough perennial that can stick it out through storm and drought, survive the trampling of careless feet and the attacks of vandals? Here is a biblical writer's view: "He grew up before him like a young plant, and like a root out of dry ground. . . . He was despised and rejected by men; a man of sorrows, and acquainted with grief. . . . He was oppressed, and he was afflicted." It is a portrait of extreme rejection and painful persecution. What can come of such a poor, precarious beginning? Not much, it would seem. Yet look at the results: "He shall see his offspring, he shall prolong his days; the will of the LORD shall prosper in his hand; he shall see the fruit of the travail of his soul and be satisfied; by his knowledge shall the righteous one, my servant, make many to be accounted righteous; and he shall bear their iniquities" (Is. 53). The person of faith outlasts all the oppressors. Faith lasts.

We remember the way it was with Jesus. His ministry began with forty days of temptation in the desert and concluded in that never to be forgotten night of testing and trial in Gethsemane and Jerusalem. Has anyone ever experienced such a relentless, merciless pounding from within and from without? First there were the cunning attempts to get him off the track, every temptation disguised as a suggestion for improvement, offered with the best of intentions to help Jesus in the ministry on which he had so naively and innocently set out. Then, at the other end, when all the temptations had failed, that brutal assault when his body was turned into a torture chamber. And we know the result: an incomprehensible kindness ("Father, forgive them..."), an unprecedented serenity ("Father, into thy hands I commit my spirit") and—resurrection.

And Paul. His life recklessly caromed from adversity to persecution and back to adversity. In one passage he looks back and summarizes: "I have been beaten times without number. I have faced death again and again. I have been beaten the regulation thirty-nine stripes by the Jews five times. I have been beaten with rods three times. I have been stoned once. I have been shipwrecked three times. I have been twenty-four hours in the open sea. In my travels I have been in constant danger from rivers, from bandits, from my own countrymen, and from pagans. I have faced danger on the high seas, danger among false Christians. I have known drudgery, exhaustion, many sleepless nights, hunger and thirst, fasting, cold and exposure. Apart from all external trials I have the daily burden of responsibility for all the churches. Do you think anyone is weak without my feeling his weakness? Does anyone have his faith upset without my burning indignation?" (2 Cor. 11:23-29 Phillips). None of that had the power to push Paul off his path. None of it convinced him that he was on the wrong way. None of it persuaded him that he had made the wrong choice years earlier on the Damascus Road. At the end of his life, among the last words he wrote, is this sentence: "Straining forward to what lies ahead, I press on toward the goal for the prize of the upward call of God in Christ Jesus" (Phil. 3:13-14).

Stick-to-it-iveness. Perseverance. Patience. The way of faith is not a fad that is taken up in one century only to be discarded in the next. It lasts. It is a way that works. It has been tested thoroughly.

Cut Cords, Withered Grass

There is an interesting line in Psalm 129 that provides a detail that is both fascinating and useful. The sentence is, "The LORD is righteous; he has cut the cords of the wicked." The previous verse provides the context for understanding the lines, "The plowers plowed upon my back; they made long their furrows." Picture Israel, the person of faith, lying stretched out, prone. The enemies hitch up their oxen and plows and begin cutting long furrows in the back of Israel. Long gashes cut into the skin and flesh, back and forth systematically, like a farmer working a field. Imagine the whole thing: the blood, the pain, the back-and-forth cruelty. And then, suddenly, the realization that there was no more hurting. The oxen were still tramping back and forth, the oxherds were still shouting their commands, but the plows were not working. "The LORD is righteous; he has cut the cords of the wicked." The harness cords, connecting plow to oxen, have been severed. The plows of persecution aren't working, and the oxherds haven't even noticed! They plod back and forth, unaware that their opposition is worthless. They are wasting their time and energy. The wicked oxherds are comic figures, solemnly and efficiently doing their impressive work, proudly puffed with self-importance thinking of what they are accomplishing historically on the back of Israel. If they ever looked behind them (which they never do—their stiff necks make that exercise too painful), they would see that their bluster and blasphemy are having no results at all: "The LORD . . . has cut the cords of the wicked."

The concluding illustration in the psalm tells a similar truth. Opposition to the people of faith is like grass on the housetops. Palestinian houses were flat topped; dirt was spread upon the roofs for insulation. Seeds would sprout and grow from this dirt but the grass didn't last; the thin soil couldn't support it. By midday the grass withered. No harvest there. No reapers upon the roofs. No one going along the road would ever look up and shout out, "Great harvest you have there. God's blessing upon you!" The illustration is a cartoon, designed to bring a smile to the people of faith.

The life of the world that is opposed or indifferent to God is barren and futile. It is plowing a field, thinking you are tramping all over God's people and cutting his purposes to ribbons, but unaware that long ago your plow was disengaged. It is naively thinking you might get a harvest of grain from that shallow patch of dirt on your rooftop. The way of the world is peppered with brief enthusiasms, like that grass on the roof, springing up so wonderfully and without effort, but as quickly withering. The way of the world is cataloged with proud, God-defying purposes, unharnessed from eternity, and therefore worthless and futile.

The Passion of Patience

There is one phrase in this psalm that good taste would prefer to delete but that honesty must deal with: "May all who hate Zion be put to shame and turned backward!" Anger seethes and pulses in the wounds. A sense of wrong has been festering. Accumulated resentment wants vindication.

However much we feel the inappropriateness of this kind of thing in a man or woman of faith, we must also admit to its authenticity. For who does not experience flashes of anger at those who make our way hard and difficult? There are times in the long obedience of Christian discipleship when we get tired and fatigue draws our tempers short. At such times to see someone flitting from one sensation to another, quitting on commitments, ducking responsibilities, bouncing from one enthusiasm to another provokes our anger—and sometimes it piques our envy. No matter that we are, on other grounds, convinced that their adulteries are an admission of boredom, that their pleasures are the shallowest of distractions from which they must return to worsening anxieties and an emptier loneliness. Still, even when we know we are doing good work which has a good future, the foolery and the enmity of these others makes a hard day harder, and anger flares.

We can't excuse the psalmist for getting angry on the grounds that he was not yet a Christian, for he had Leviticus to read: "You shall not hate your brother in your heart. . . . You shall not take vengeance or bear any grudge against the sons of your own people, but you shall love your neighbor as yourself" (Lev. 19:17-18). And he had Exodus: "If you meet your enemy's ox or his ass going astray, you shall bring it back to him. If you see the ass of one who hates you lying under its burden, you shall refrain from leaving him with it, you shall help him to lift it up" (Ex. 23:4-5). And he had Proverbs: "Do not rejoice when your enemy falls, and let not your heart be glad when he stumbles" (Prov. 24:17). When Jesus said "love your enemies," he added nothing to what this psalmist already had before him.

So we will not make excuses for the psalmist's vindictiveness. What we will do is admire its energy, for it is apathetic, sluggish neutrality that is death to perseverance, acts like a virus in the bloodstream and enervates the muscles of discipleship. The person who makes excuses for the hypocrites and rationalizes the excesses of the wicked, who loses a sense of opposition to sin, who obscures the difference between faith and denial, grace and selfishness—*that* is the person to be wary of. For if there is not all that much difference between the way of faith and the ways of the world, there is not much use in making any effort to stick to it. We drift on the tides of convenience. We float on fashions.

It is in the things that we care about that we are capable of expressing anger. A parent sees a child dart out into a roadway and narrowly miss being hit by a car, and angrily yells at the child, at the driver—at both. The anger may not be the most appropriate expression of concern, but it is evidence of concern. Indifference would be somehow inhuman.

And so here. The psalms are not sung by perfect pilgrims. They made their mistakes, just as we make ours. *Perseverance* does not mean "perfect." It means that we keep going. We do not quit when we find that we are not yet mature and that there is a long journey still before us. We get caught yelling at our wives, at our husbands, at our friends, at our employers, at our employees, at our children. Our yelling (though not all of it!) means we care about something: we care about God; we care about the ways of the kingdom; we care about morality, about justice, about righteousness. The way of faith centers and absorbs our lives and when someone makes the way difficult, throws stumbling blocks in the path of the innocent, creates difficulties for those young in faith and unpracticed in obedience, there is anger: "May all who hate Zion be put to shame and turned backward!"

For perseverance **is** not resignation, putting up with things the way they are, staying in the same old rut year after year after year, or being a doormat for people to wipe their feet on. Endurance is not a desperate hanging on but a traveling from strength to strength. There is nothing fatigued or humdrum in Isaiah, nothing flatfooted in Jesus, nothing jejune in Paul. Perseverance is triumphant and alive. The psalmist lived among prophets and priests who dealt with his vindictive spirit and nurtured him toward a better way of treating the wicked than calling down curses on them, learning what Charles Williams once described as the "passion of patience." We are in a similar apprenticeship. But we will not learn it by swallowing our sense of outrage on the one hand, or, on the other, excusing all wickedness as a neurosis. We will do it by offering up our anger to God who trains us in creative love.

God Sticks with Us

The cornerstone sentence of Psalm 129 is, "The LORD is righteous." When the Bible says that God is righteous it is not saying that he is always right (although it, of course, assumes that) but that he is always in right relation to us. The word does not mean that he corresponds to some abstract ideal of the right, it speaks of a personal right relationship between Creator and his creation. ". . . Righteous is out and out a term denoting relationship, and that it does this in the sense of referring to a real relationship between two parties . . . and not to the relationship of an object under consideration to an idea."[1]

That the "LORD is righteous" is the reason that Christians can look back over a long life, crisscrossed with cruelties, unannounced tragedies, unexpected setbacks, sufferings, disappointments, depressions—look back across all that and see it as a road of blessing and make a song out of what we see. "Sorely have they afflicted me from my youth, yet they have not prevailed against me." God sticks to his relationship. He establishes a personal relationship with us and stays with it. The central reality for Christians is the personal, unalterable, persevering commitment that God makes to us. Perseverance is not the result of *our* determination, it is the result of God's faithfulness. We survive in the way of faith not because we have extraordinary stamina but because God is righteous. Christian discipleship is a process of paying more and more attention to God's righteousness and less and less attention to our own; finding the meaning of our lives not by probing our moods and motives and morals but by believing in God's will and purposes; making a map of the faithfulness of God, not charting the rise and fall of our enthusiasms. It is out of such a reality that we acquire perseverance.

This is what the writer of the New Testament letter to the Hebrew Christians did. He sang a litany of people who lived by faith, that is, people who centered their lives on the righteous God who stuck by them through thick and thin in such a way that they were able to persevere. They lived with uncommon steadiness of purpose and with a most admirable integrity. None of them lived without sin. They all made their share of mistakes and engaged in episodes of disobedience and rebellion. But God stuck with them so consistently and surely that they learned how to stick with God. Out of that litany comes this call: "Let us run with perseverance the race that is set before us, looking to Jesus the pioneer and perfecter of our faith, who for the joy that was set before him endured the cross, despising the shame, and is seated at the right hand of the throne of God" (Heb. 12:1-2).

Some of those early Christians to whom he wrote had been complaining, apparently, that life was too rough for them. They couldn't hold out any longer (complaints that are, from time to time, heard in every congregation). They didn't see the use in believing in a God they never saw, serving a God who didn't give them what they want, trusting a God who let babies die and good people suffer. There is just a touch of irony in the words their pastor addressed to them: "In your struggle against sin you have not yet resisted to the point of shedding your blood." Quit your complaining. Take a look at the pilgrim road and see where you have come from and where you are going. Take up the refrains of the great song. " 'Sorely have they afflicted us from our youth,' let Israel now say"—come now, all of you sing it—" 'Sorely have they afflicted us from our youth, yet they have not prevailed against us.' "

Purposes Last

The reason why our childhoods were one enthusiasm after another was that we hadn't yet found an organizing center for our lives and a goal that would demand our all and our best. The Christian faith is the discovery of that center in the righteous God. Christian discipleship is a decision to walk in his ways, steadily and firmly, and then finding that the way integrates all our interests, passions and gifts, our human needs and our eternal aspirations. It is the way of life we were created for. There are endless challenges in it to keep us on the growing edge of faith; there is always a righteous God with us to make it possible for us to persevere.

In Charles Williams's delightful, brief drama, *Grab and Grace*, there is a dialog between Grace and a man who is dabbling in religion, trying out different experiences, "into yoga one week, buddhism the next, spiritualism the next." Grace mentions the Holy Spirit. The man says,

"The Holy Spirit? Good. We will ask him to come while I am in the mood, which passes so quickly and then all is so dull."

And Grace answers:

"Sir, purposes last."

12: Hope

"I Wait for the LORD, My Soul Waits"

Out of the depths I cry to thee, O LORD!
  Lord, hear my voice!
Let thy ears be attentive
  to the voice of my supplications!

If thou, O LORD, shouldst mark iniquities,
  Lord, who could stand?
But there is forgiveness with thee,
  that thou mayest be feared.

I wait for the LORD, my soul waits,
  and in his word I hope;
my soul waits for the LORD
  more than watchmen for the morning,
  more than watchmen for the morning.

O Israel, hope in the LORD!
  For with the LORD there is steadfast love,
  and with him is plenteous redemption.
And he will redeem Israel
  from all his iniquities.

Psalm 130

Hope is a projection of the imagination; so is despair. Despair all too readily embraces the ills it foresees; hope is an energy and arouses the mind to explore every possibility to combat them. . . . In response to hope the imagination is aroused to picture every possible issue, to try every door, to fit together even the most heterogeneous pieces in the puzzle. After the solution has been found it is difficult to recall the steps taken—so many of them are just below the level of consciousness.

Thornton Wilder

To be human is to be in trouble. Job's anguish is our epigraph: "Man is born to trouble as the sparks fly upward." Suffering is a characteristic of the personal. Animals can be hurt, but they do not suffer. The earth can be ravaged, still it cannot suffer. Man and woman, alone in the creation, suffer. For suffering is pain *plus:* physical or emotional pain *plus* the awareness that our own worth as people is threatened, that our own value as creatures made in the dignity of God is called into question, that our own destiny as eternal souls is jeopardized. Are we to be, finally, nothing? Are we to be discarded? Are we to be rejects in the universe and thrown onto the garbage dump of humanity because our bodies degenerate or our emotions malfunction or our minds become confused or our families find fault with us or society avoids us? Any one of these things or, as is more likely, a combination of them, can put us in what Psalm 130 calls the depths.

A Christian is a person who decides to face and live through suffering. If we do not make that decision, we are endangered on every side. A man or woman of faith who fails to acknowledge and deal with suffering becomes, at last, either a cynic or a melancholic or a suicide. Psalm 130 grapples mightily with suffering, sings its way through it, and provides usable experience for those who are committed to traveling the way of faith to God through Jesus Christ.

Giving Dignity to Suffering
The psalm begins in pain: "Out of the depths I cry to thee, O LORD! Lord, hear my voice! Let thy ears be attentive to the voice of my supplications!" The psalm is anguished prayer.

By setting the anguish out in the open and voicing it as a prayer, the psalm gives dignity to our suffering. It does not look on suffering as something slightly embarrassing which must be hushed up and locked in a closet (where it finally becomes a skeleton) because this sort of thing shouldn't happen to a real person of faith. And it doesn't treat it as a puzzle that must be explained, and therefore turn it over to theologians or philosophers to work out an answer. Suffering is set squarely, openly, passionately before God. It is acknowledged and expressed. It is described and lived.

If the psalm did nothing more than that, it would be a prize, for it is difficult to find anyone in our culture who will respect us when we suffer. We live in a time when everyone's goal is to be perpetually healthy and constantly happy, and if any one of us fails to live up to the standards that are advertised as normative, we are labeled as a problem to be solved and a host of well-intentioned people rush to try out various cures on us. Or we are looked on as an enigma to be unraveled in which case we are subjected to endless discussions in which our lives are examined by zealous researchers for the clue that will account for our lack of health or happiness. Ivan Illich, in a recent interview, said: "You know, there is an American myth that denies suffering and the sense of pain. It acts as if they *should* not be, and hence it devalues the *experience* of suffering. But this myth denies our encounter with reality."[1]

The gospel offers a different view of suffering: in suffering we enter *the depths;* we are at the heart of things; we are near to where Christ was on the cross. P. T. Forsyth wrote: "The depth is simply the height inverted, as sin is the index of moral grandeur. The cry is not only truly human, but divine as well. God is deeper than the deepest depth in man. He is holier than our deepest sin is deep. There is no depth so deep to us as when God reveals his holiness in dealing with our sin. . . . [And so] think more of the depth of God than the depth of your cry. The worst thing that can happen to a man is to have no God to cry to out of the depth."[2]

Israel teaches us to respond to suffering as reality, not deny it as illusion, and leads us to face it with faith, not avoid it out of terror. The psalm in this way is representative of Israel which "took a supremely realistic view of life's sufferings and dangers, saw herself as exposed to them vulnerably and without defence, and showed little talent for fleeing from them into ideologies of any kind. Rather, concepts of her faith directed her to bring these actual experiences of her daily life into connexion with Jahweh. In her older period, indeed, she lacked any aptitude for the doctrinaire: she possessed, rather, an exceptional strength to face up even to negative realities, to recognize and not to repress them, even when she was spiritually unable to master them in any way. It is to this realism, which allowed every event its own inevitability and validity . . . that the narrative art of the OT, especially in its earlier form, owes its darksome grandeur."[3]

And so we find in Psalm 130 not so much as a trace of those things that are so common among us, which rob us of our humanity when we suffer and make the pain so much more terrible to bear. No glib smart answers. No lectures on our misfortunes in which we are hauled into a classroom and given graduate courses in suffering. No hasty, Band-Aid treatments covering up our trouble so that the rest of society does not have to look at it. Neither prophets nor priests nor psalmists offer quick cures for the suffering: we don't find any of them telling us to take a vacation, use this drug, get a hobby. Nor do they ever engage in publicity cover-ups, the plastic smile propaganda campaigns that hide trouble behind a billboard of positive thinking. None of that: the suffering is held up and proclaimed—and prayed.

Not that Christians celebrate suffering—we don't make a religion out of it. We are not masochists who think we are being holy when we are hurting, who think personal misery is a sign of exceptional righteousness. There is some suffering in which we get involved that is useless and unnecessary; but there is adequate common-sense wisdom in Christian ways which prevents us from suffering for the wrong reasons if only we will pay attention to it. Henri Nouwen wrote, "Many people suffer because of the false supposition on which they have based their lives. That supposition is that there should be no fear or loneliness, no confusion or doubt. But these sufferings can only be dealt with creatively when they are understood as wounds integral to our human condition. Therefore ministry is a very *confronting* service. It does not allow people to live with illusions of immortality and wholeness. It keeps reminding others that they are mortal and broken, but also that with the recognition of this condition, liberation starts."[4] George MacDonald put it with epigrammatic force when he wrote, "The Son of God suffered unto the death, not that men might not suffer, but that their sufferings might be like His."[5]

The second important thing that Psalm 130 does is to immerse the suffering in God—all the suffering is spoken in the form of prayer, which means that God is taken seriously as a personal and concerned being. There are sentences in the psalm which show specific knowledge of the character of God as a personal redeemer: God is personal so that we may have an intimate relation with him; God is redeemer so that we may be helped by him. There is *meaning to* our lives and there is *salvation for* our lives, a truth summed up by Forsyth when he said, "Our very pain is a sign of God's remembrance of us, for it would be much worse if we were left in ghastly isolation."[6]

Eight times the name of God is used in the psalm. We find, as we observe how God is addressed, that he is under-

stood as one who forgives sin, who comes to those who wait
and hope for him, who is characterized by steadfast love
and plenteous redemption, and who will redeem Israel.
God makes a difference. God acts positively toward his
people. God is not indifferent. He is not rejecting. He is not
ambivilant or dilatory. He does not act arbitrarily in fits and
starts. He is not stingy, providing only for bare survival.
Karl Barth describes God in this regard: "The free inclination of God to His creature, denoted in the Biblical witness
by grace, takes place under the presupposition that the
creature is in distress and that God's intention is to espouse
his cause and to grant him assistance in his extremity. Because grace, the gracious love of God, consists in this inclination, it is, and therefore God Himself is, merciful; God's
very being is mercy. The mercy of God lies in His readiness
to share in sympathy the distress of another, a readiness
which springs from His inmost nature and stamps all His
being and doing. It lies, therefore, in His will, springing
from the depths of His nature and characterising it, to take
the initiative Himself for the removal of this distress. For
the fact that God participates in it by sympathy implies that
He is really present in its midst, and this means again that
He wills that it should not be, that He wills therefore to remove it."[7]

And this, of course, is why we are able to face, acknowledge, accept and live through suffering, for we know that it
can never be ultimate, it can never constitute the bottom
line. God is at the foundation and God is at the boundaries.
God seeks the hurt, maimed, wandering and lost. God woos
the rebellious and confused. If God were different than he
is, not one of us would have a leg to stand on: "If thou, O
LORD, shouldst mark iniquities, Lord, who could stand? But
there is forgiveness with thee, that thou mayest be feared."
Because of the forgiveness we have a place to stand. We
stand in confident awe before God, not in terrorized despair.

Employed to Wait

Such are the two great realities of Psalm 130: suffering is
real, God is real. Suffering is a mark of our existential
authenticity; God is proof of our essential and eternal humanity. We accept suffering; we believe in God. The acceptance and the belief both come from "the depths."

But there is more than a description of reality here, there
is a procedure for participating in it. The program is given
in two words: *wait* and *hope*. The words are at the center
of the psalm. "I wait for the LORD, my soul waits, and in his
word I hope; my soul waits for the LORD more than watchmen for the morning, more than watchmen for the morning. O Israel, hope in the LORD!"

The words *wait* and *hope* are connected with the image of
the watchmen waiting through the night for the dawn. The
connection provides important insights for the person in
trouble who asks, "But surely, there is something for me to
do!" The answer is yes, there is something for you to do, or
more exactly there is someone you can be; be a watchman.

A watchman is an important person, but he doesn't do
very much. The massive turning of the earth, the immense
energies released by the sun—all that goes on apart from
him. He does nothing to influence or control such things:
he is a watchman. He knows the dawn is coming; there are
no doubts concerning that. Meanwhile he is alert to dangers, he comforts restless children or animals until it is time
to work or play again in the light of day.

I was once a watchman. I worked from 10 P.M. until
6 A.M. in a building in New York City. My work as a night
watchman was combined with that of elevator operator, but
the elevator work petered out about midnight. After that I
sat and read, dozed or studied. There were assorted night
people in the neighborhood who would stop in through
the night hours and visit with me: strange, bizarre people
with wonderful stories. I will know how much of what

I heard from them was fact and how much fiction: a failed millionaire obsessed with communist plots responsible for his demise, a South American adventurer now too old to tramp the remote jungles and mountains, a couple of streetwalkers who on slow nights would sit and talk about God and the worth of their souls.

I did that for an entire year. I stayed awake, I studied, I learned. I visited and gossiped. And I waited for the dawn. Dawn always came. The people who employed me thought it was worth several dollars an hour for me to wait through the night and watch for the morning. But I never did anything, never constructed anything, never made anything happen. I waited. I hoped.

If I had not known that there were others in charge of the building, I might not have been content to just be a watchman and collect my pay. If I were not confident that the building had an owner who cared about it, if I did not know that there was a building engineer who kept it in good order and repair, if I did not know that there were hundreds of people in the building who were going about their work everyday quite capably ... if I had not known these things, I might not have been so relaxed in making idle gossip with women of the night and old men of storied pasts.

Nor would the psalmist have been content to be a watchman if he were not sure of God. The psalmist's and the Christian's waiting and hoping is based on the conviction that God is actively involved in his creation and vigorously at work in redemption.

Waiting does not mean doing nothing. It is not fatalistic resignation. It means going about our assigned tasks, confident that God will provide the meaning and the conclusions. It is not compelled to work away at keeping up appearances with a bogus spirituality. It is the opposite of desperate and panicky manipulations, of scurrying and worrying.

And hoping is not dreaming. It is not spinning an illusion of fantasy to protect us from our boredom or our pain. It means a confident alert expectation that God will do what he said he will do. It is imagination put in the harness of faith. It is a willingness to let him do it his way and in his time. It is the opposite of making plans that we demand that God put into effect, telling him both how and when to do it. That is not hoping in God but bullying God. "I wait for the LORD, my soul waits, and in his word I hope; my soul waits for the LORD more than watchmen for the morning, more than watchmen for the morning."

An Eye Specialist and a Painter

When we suffer we attract counselors as money attracts thieves. Everybody has an idea of what we did wrong to get ourselves into such trouble and a prescription for what we can do to get out of it. We are flooded first with sympathy and then with advice, and when we don't come around quickly we are abandoned as a hopeless case. But none of that is what we need. We need hope. We need to know that we are in relation to God. We need to know that suffering is part of what it means to be human and not something alien. We need to know where *we* are and where *God* is. We need an eye specialist rather, than, say, a painter. A painter tries to convey to us with the aid of his brush and palette a picture of the world as he sees it; an ophthalmologist tries to enable us to see the world as it really is.

There is a passage in George MacDonald's novel *The Princess and Curdie* that tells us that when Curdie reaches the castle, he sees the great staircase and he knows that to reach the tower he must go further. The narrator takes the occasion to say that "those who work well in the depths more easily understand the heights, for indeed in their true nature they are one and the same."[8]

For the person who suffers, has suffered, or will suffer

Psalm 130 is essential equipment, for it convinces us that the big difference is not in what people suffer but in the way they suffer. ("The same shaking that makes fetid water stink makes perfume issue a more pleasant odor."⁹) The psalm does not exhort us to put up with suffering; it does not explain it or explain it away. It is, rather, a powerful demonstration that our place in the depths is not out of bounds from God. We see that whatever or whoever got us in trouble cannot separate us from God, for "there is forgiveness with thee." We are persuaded that God's way with us is redemption and that the redemption, not the suffering, is ultimate.

The depths have a bottom; the heights are boundless. Knowing that, we are helped to go ahead and learn the skills of waiting and hoping by which God is given room to work out our salvation and develop our faith while we fix our attention on his ways of grace and resurrection.

13: Humility

"My Eyes Are Not Raised Too High"

O LORD, my heart is not lifted up,
my eyes are not raised too high;
I do not occupy myself with things
too great and too marvelous for me.
But I have calmed and quieted my soul,
like a child quieted at its mother's breast;
like a child that is quieted is my soul.

O Israel, hope in the LORD
from this time forth and for evermore.

Psalm 131

Humility is the obverse side of
confidence in God, whereas pride is the
obverse side of confidence in self.

John Baillie

Christian faith needs continuous maintenance. It requires attending to. "If you leave a thing alone you leave it to a torrent of change. If you leave a white post alone it will soon be a black post."[1]

Every spring in my neighborhood a number of people prune their bushes and trees. It is an annual practice with people who care about growing things. It is also one of those acts which an outsider, one who does not understand how growth works, almost always misunderstands, for it always looks like an act of mutilation. It appears that you are ruining the plant, when, in fact, you are helping it. We have a rosebush that hasn't been pruned for several years. When it first bloomed the roses were full and vigorous. Last summer the plant was larger than ever. The vines ranged up to the roof on a trellis I had made. I anticipated more roses than ever. But I was disappointed. The blossoms were small and scrawny. The branches had gotten too far from their roots. The plant couldn't grow a good blossom. It needed a good pruning.

Psalm 131 is a maintenance psalm. It is functional to the person of faith as pruning is functional to the gardener: it gets rid of that which looks good to those who don't know any better, and reduces the distance between our hearts and their roots in God.

The two things that Psalm 131 prunes away are unruly ambition and infantile dependency, what we might call getting too big for our breeches, and refusing to cut the apron strings. Both of these tendencies can easily be supposed to be virtues, especially by those who are not conversant with Christian ways. If we are not careful, we will be encouraging the very things that will ruin us. We are in special and constant need of expert correction. We need pruning. Jesus said, "Every branch of mine that bears no fruit, he takes away, and every branch that does bear fruit he prunes, that it may bear more fruit" (Jn. 15:2). More than once our Lord the Spirit has used Psalm 131 to do this important work among his people. As we gain a familiarity with and an understanding of the psalm, he will be able to use it that way with us "that we may bear more fruit."

Aspiration Gone Crazy

"O LORD, my heart is not lifted up, my eyes are not raised too high; I do not occupy myself with things too great and too marvelous for me. But I have calmed and quieted my soul."

These lines are enormously difficult for us to comprehend—not that they are difficult to understand with our minds, for the words are all plain, but difficult to grasp with our emotions, feeling their truth. All cultures throw certain stumbling blocks in the way of those who pursue gospel realities. It is sheerest fantasy to suppose that we would have had an easier time of it as Christian believers if we were in another land or another time. It is no easier to be a Chinese Christian than to be a Spanish Christian than to be a Russian Christian than to be a Brazilian Christian than to be an American Christian—nor more difficult. The way of faith deals with realities in whatever time or whatever culture.

But there are differences from time to time and from p.acc to place which cause special problems. For instance, when an ancient temptation or trial becomes an approved feature in the culture, a way of life that is expected and encouraged, Christians have a stumbling block put before them that is hard to recognize for what it is, for it has been made into a monument, gilded with bronze and bathed in decorative lights. It has become an object of veneration. But the plain fact is that it is right in the middle of the road of faith, obstructing discipleship. For all its fancy dress and honored position it is still a stumbling block.

One temptation that has received this treatment in Western civilization, with some special flourishes in America, is ambition. Our culture encourages and rewards ambition without qualification. We are surrounded by a way of life in which betterment is understood as expansion, as acquisition, as fame. Everyone wants to get more. To be on top, no matter what it is the top of, is admired. There is nothing recent about the temptation. It is the oldest sin in the book, the one that got Adam thrown out of the garden and Lucifer tossed out of heaven. What is fairly new about it is the general admiration and approval that it receives.

The old story of Doctor Faustus used to be well known and appreciated as a warning. John Faustus became impatient with the limitations placed upon him in his study of law, of medicine, of theology. No matter how much he learned in these fields he found he was always in the service of something greater than he was—of justice, of healing, of God. He chafed in the service and wanted out: he wanted to be in control, to break out of the limits of the finite. So he became an adept in magic by which he was able to defy the laws of physics, the restrictions of morality and relations with God and use his knowledge in these fields for his own pleasures and purposes. In order to bring it off, though, he had to make a pact with the devil which permitted him to act for the next twenty-four years in a godlike way— living without limits, being in control instead of being in relationship, exercising power instead of practicing love. But at the end of the twenty-four years was damnation.

For generations this story has been told and retold by poets and playwrights and novelists (Goethe, Marlowe, Mann) warning people against abandoning the glorious position of being a person created in the image of God and attempting the foolhardy adventure of trying to be a god on our own. But now something alarming has happened. There have always been Faustian characters, people in the community who embarked on a way of arrogance and power; now our entire culture is Faustian. We are caught up in a way of life which, instead of delighting in finding out the meaning of God and searching out the conditions in which human qualities can best be realized, recklessly seeks ways to circumvent nature, arrogantly defies personal relationships and names God only in curses. The legend of Faustus, useful for so long in pointing out the folly of a god-defying pride, now is practically unrecognizable because the assumptions of our whole society (our educational models, our economic expectations, even our popular religion) are Faustian.

It is difficult to recognize pride as a sin when it is held up on every side as a virtue, urged as profitable, and rewarded as an achievement. What is described in Scripture as the basic sin, the sin of taking things into your own hands, being your own god, grabbing what is there while you can get it, is now described as basic wisdom: improve yourself by whatever means you are able; get ahead regardless of the price, take care of me first. For a limited time it works. But at the end the devil has his due. There is damnation.

It is additionally difficult to recognize unruly ambition as a sin because it has a kind of superficial relationship to the virtue of aspiration—an impatience with mediocrity, and a dissatisfaction with all things created until we are at home with the Creator, the hopeful striving for the best God has for us—the kind of thing Paul expressed: "I press on toward the goal for the prize of the upward call of God in Christ Jesus" (Phil. 3:14). But if we take the energies that make for aspiration and remove God from the picture, replacing him with our own crudely sketched self-portrait, we end up with ugly arrogance. Robert Browning's fine line on aspiration, "A man's reach should exceed his grasp, or what's a heaven for?" has been distorted to "Reach for the skies and grab everything that isn't nailed down." Ambition is aspiration gone crazy. Aspiration is the channeled, creative energy that moves us to growth in Christ, shaping goals in the Spirit. Ambition takes these same energies for growth and development and uses them to make something tawdry and cheap, sweatily knocking together a Babel when we could be vacationing in Eden. Calvin comments, "Those who yield themselves up to the influence of ambition will soon lose themselves in a labyrinth of perplexity."[2]

Our lives are only lived well when they are lived in terms of their creation, with God loving and us being loved, with God making and us being made, with God revealing and us understanding, with God commanding and us responding. Being a Christian means accepting the terms of creation, accepting God as our maker and redeemer, and growing day by day into an increasingly glorious creature in Christ, developing joy, experiencing love, maturing in peace. By the grace of Christ we experience the marvel of being made in the image of God. If we reject this way the only alternative is to attempt the hopelessly fourth-rate, embarrassingly awkward imitation of God made in the image of man.

Both revelation and experience (Genesis and Goethe) show it to be the wrong way, and so the psalmist is wise to see it and sing, "O LORD, my heart is not lifted up, my eyes are not raised too high; I do not occupy myself with things too great and too marvelous for me. But I have calmed and quieted my soul." I will not try to run my own life or the lives of others; that is God's business, I will not pretend to invent the meaning of the universe; I will accept what God has shown its meaning to be; I will not noisily strut about demanding that I be treated as the center of my family or my neighborhood or my work, but seek to dis-

cover where I fit and do what I am good at. The soul, clamorously crying out for attention and arrogantly parading its
importance, is calmed and quieted so that it can be itself,
truly.

As Content as a Child

But if we are not to be proud, clamorous, arrogant persons,
what are we to be? Mousy, cringing, insecure ones? Well,
not quite. Having realized the dangers of pride, the sin of
thinking too much of ourselves, we are suddenly in danger
of another mistake, that of thinking too little of ourselves.
There are some who conclude that since the great Christian
temptation is to try to be everything, the perfect Christian
solution is to be nothing. And so we have the problem of the
doormat Christian and the dishrag saint: the person upon
whom everyone walks and wipes their feet, the person who
is used by others to clean up the mess of everyday living
and then discarded. These people then compensate for
their poor lives by weepily clinging to God, hoping to make
up for the miseries of everyday life by dreaming of luxuries in heaven.

Christian faith is not neurotic dependency but childlike
trust. We do not have a God who forever indulges our
whims but a God whom we trust with our destinies. The
Christian is not a naive, innocent infant who has no identity
apart from a feeling of being comforted and protected and
catered to but a person who has discovered an identity that
is given by God which can be enjoyed best and fully in a
voluntary trust in God. We do not cling to God desperately
out of fear and the panic of insecurity; we come to him
freely in faith and love.

Our Lord gave us the picture of the child as a model for
Christian faith (Mk. 10:14-16) not because of the child's
helplessness but because of the child's willingness to be led,
to be taught, to be blessed. God does not reduce us to a set

of Pavlovian reflexes in which we mindlessly worship and pray and obey on signal; he establishes us with a dignity in which we are free to receive his word, his gifts, his grace.

The psalm shows great genius at this point and describes a relationship which is completely attractive. The translators of the Jerusalem Bible have retained the literalism of the Hebrew metaphor: "Enough for me to keep my soul tranquil and quiet like a child in its mother's arms, as content as a child that has been weaned." The last phrase, "as a child that has been weaned," creates a completely new, unguessed reality. The Christian is "not like an infant crying loudly for his mother's breast, but like a weaned child that quietly rests by his mother's side, happy in being with her. . . . No desire now comes between him and his God; for he is sure that God knows what he needs before he asks him. And just as the child gradually breaks off the habit of regarding his mother only as a means of satisfying his own desires and learns to love her for her own sake, so the worshipper after a struggle has reached an attitude of mind in which he desires God for himself and not as a means of fulfillment of his own wishes. His life's centre of gravity has shifted. He now rests no longer in himself but in God."[3]

The transition from a sucking infant to a weaned child, from squalling baby to quiet son or daughter, is not smooth. It is stormy and noisy. It is no easy thing to quiet yourself: sooner may a person calm the sea or rule the wind or tame a tiger, than quiet oneself. It is pitched battle. The baby is denied expected comforts and flies into rages or sinks into sulks. There are sobs and struggles. The infant is facing its first great sorrow and it is in sore distress. But "to the weaned child his mother is his comfort though she has denied him comfort. It is a blessed mark of growth out of spiritual infancy when we can forego the joys which once appeared to be essential, and can find our solace in him who denies them to us."[4]

Many who have traveled this way of faith have described the transition from an infantile faith that grabs at God out of desperation to a mature faith that responds to God out of love . . . "as content as a child that has been weaned." Often our conscious Christian lives do begin at points of desperation, and God, of course, does not refuse to meet our needs. There are heavenly comforts that break through our despair and persuade us that "all will be well and all manner of things will be well." The early stages of Christian belief are not infrequently marked with miraculous signs and exhilarations of spirit. But as discipleship continues the sensible comforts gradually disappear. For God does not want us neurotically dependent upon him but willingly trustful in him. And so he weans us. The period of infancy will not be sentimentally extended beyond what is necessary. The time of weaning is very often noisy and marked with misunderstandings: "I no longer feel like I did when I was first a Christian. Does that mean I am no longer a Christian? Has God abandoned me? Have I done something terribly wrong?"

The answer is, "Neither: God hasn't abandoned you and you haven't done anything wrong. You are being weaned. The apron strings have been cut. You are free to come to God or not come to him. You are, in a sense, on your own with an open invitation to listen and receive and enjoy our Lord."

The last line of the psalm addresses this quality of newly acquired freedom: "O Israel, hope in the LORD from this time forth and for evermore." Choose to be with him; elect his presence; aspire to his ways; respond to his love.

The Plain Way

When Charles Spurgeon preached this psalm he said that it "is one of the shortest Psalms to read, but one of the longest to learn."[5] We are always, it seems, reeling from one side of the road to the other as we travel in the way of faith. At one turning of the road we are presented with awesome problems and terrifying emergencies. We rise to the challenge, take things into our own hands to become master of the situation, telling God, "Thank you, but get lost. We'll take care of this one ourselves." At the next turning we are overwhelmed and run in a panic to some kind of infantile religion that will solve all our problems for us, freeing us of the burden of thinking and the difficulty of choosing. We are, alternately, rebellious runaways and whining babies. Worse, we have numerous experts, so-called, encouraging us to pursue one or the other of these ways.

The experts in our society who offer to help us have a kind of general-staff mentality, from which massive, top-down solutions are issued to solve our problems. Then when the solutions don't work, we get mired in the nothing-can-be-done swamp. We are first incited into being grandiose and then intimidated into being infantile. But there is another way, the plain way of quiet, Christian humility. We need pruning. Cut back to our roots, we then learn this psalm and discover the quietness of the weaned child, the tranquillity of maturing trust. It is such a minute psalm that many have overlooked it, but for all its brevity and lack of pretense it is essential. For every Christian encounters problems of growth and difficulties of development.

A number of years ago Peter Marin made an incisive observation that was very much in the spirit of Psalm 131. "There are cultural conditions," he wrote, "for which there are no solutions, turnings of the soul so profound and complex that no system can absorb or contain them. How could one have 'solved' the Reformation? Or first-century Rome? One makes accommodations and adjustments, one dreams about the future and makes plans to save us all, but in spite of all that, because of it, what seems more important are the private independent acts that become more necessary

every day: the ways we find as private persons to restore to
one another the strengths we should have now—whether to
make the kind of revolution we need or to survive the re-
pression that seems likely . . . what saves us as men and
women is always a kind of witness: the quality of our own
acts and lives."[6]

And that is what Psalm 131 nurtures: a quality of calm
confidence and quiet strength which knows the difference
between unruly arrogance and faithful aspiration, knows
how to discriminate between infantile dependency and
childlike trust, and chooses to aspire and to trust—and to
sing, "Enough for me to keep my soul tranquil and quiet
like a child in its mother's arms, as content as a child that
has been weaned."

14: Obedience

"How He Swore to the LORD"

Remember, O LORD, in David's favor,
  all the hardships he endured;
how he swore to the LORD
  and vowed to the Mighty One of Jacob,
*"I will **not** enter my house*
  *or **get into** my bed;*
I will not give sleep to my eyes
  or slumber to my eyelids,
until I find a place for the LORD,
  a dwelling place for the Mighty One of Jacob."

Lo, we heard of it in Ephrathah,
  we found it in the fields of Jaar.
"Let us go to his dwelling place;
  let us worship at his footstool!"

Arise, O LORD, and go to thy resting place,
  thou and the ark of thy might.
Let thy priests be clothed with righteousness,
  and let thy saints shout for joy.
For thy servant David's sake
  do not turn away the face of thy anointed one.

The LORD swore to David a sure oath
  from which he will not turn back:
"One of the sons of your body

I will set on your throne.
If your sons keep my covenant
  and my testimonies which I shall teach them,
their sons also for ever
  shall sit upon your throne."

For the LORD has chosen Zion;
  he has desired it for his habitation:
"This is my resting place for ever;
  here I will dwell, for I have desired it.
I will abundantly bless her provisions;
  I will satisfy her poor with bread.
Her priests I will clothe with salvation,
  and her saints will shout for joy.
There I will make a horn to sprout for David;
  I have prepared a lamp for my anointed,
His enemies I will clothe with shame,
  but upon himself his crown will shed its luster."

Psalm 132

True knowledge of God is born out of obedience.

John Calvin

An incident took place a few years ago that has acquired the force of a parable for me. I had a minor operation on my nose and was in my hospital room recovering. Even though the surgery was minor, the pain was great and I was full of misery. Late in the afternoon a man was assigned to the other bed in my room. He was to have a tonsillectomy the next day. He was young, about twenty-two years old, good looking and friendly. He came over to me, put out his hand, and said, "Hi, my name is Kelly. What happened to you?" I was in no mood for friendly conversation, did not return the handshake, grunted my name and said that I had gotten my nose broken. He got the message that I did not want to talk, pulled the curtain between our beds and let me alone. Later in the evening his friends were visiting and I heard him say, "There's a man in the next bed who is a prize fighter; he got his nose broken in a championship fight." He went on to embellish the story for the benefit of his friends.

Later in the evening as I was feeling better I said, "Kelly, you misunderstood what I said. I'm not a prize fighter. The nose was broken years ago in a basketball game and I am just now getting it fixed."

"Well, what then do you do?"

"I'm a pastor."

"Oh," he said and turned away; I was no longer an interesting subject.

In the morning he woke me: "Peterson, Peterson—wake up." I groggily came awake and asked what he wanted. "I want you to pray for me; I'm scared." And so, before he was taken to surgery, I went to his bedside and prayed for him.

When he was brought back a couple of hours later, a nurse came and said, "Kelly, I am going to give you an injection that should take care of any pain that you might have."

In twenty minutes or so he began to groan, "I hurt. I can't stand it. I'm going to die."

I rang for the nurse and, when she came, said, "Nurse, I don't think that shot did any good; why don't you give him another one." She didn't acknowledge my credentials for making such a suggestion, told me curtly that she would oversee the medical care of the patient, turned on her heel and, a little abruptly I thought, left. Meanwhile Kelly continued to vent his agony.

After another half an hour he began to hallucinate, and having lost touch with reality began to shout, "Peterson, pray for me; can't you see I'm dying! Peterson, pray for me." His shouts brought nurses and doctors and orderlies running. They held him down and quieted him with the injection that I had prescribed earlier.

The parabolic force of the incident is this: when the man was scared he wanted me to pray for him, and when the man was crazy he wanted me to pray for him, but in between, during the hours of so-called normalcy, he didn't want anything to do with a pastor. What Kelly betrayed *in extremis* is all many people know of religion: a religion to help them with their fears but which is forgotten when the fears are taken care of; a religion made of moments of craziness but which is remote and shadowy in the clear light of the sun and in the routines of every day. The most religious places in the world, as a matter of fact, are not churches but battlefields and mental hospitals. You are much more likely to find passionate prayer in a foxhole than in a church pew; and you will certainly find more otherwordly visions and supernatural voices in a mental hospital than you will in a church.

Stable not Petrified

Nevertheless we Christians don't go to either place to nurture our faith. We don't deliberately put ourselves in places of fearful danger to evoke heartfelt prayer, and we don't put ourselves in psychiatric wards so we can be around those who clearly see visions of heaven and hell, and distinctly hear the voice of God. What most Christians do is come to church, a place that is fairly safe and moderately predictable. For we have an instinct for health and sanity in our faith. We don't seek out death-defying situations, and we avoid mentally unstable teachers. But in doing that we don't get what some people seem to want very much, namely, a religion that makes us safe at all costs, certifying us as inoffensive to our neighbors and guaranteeing us as good credit risks to the banks. It would be simply awful to find that as we grew in Christ we became dull, that as we developed in discipleship we became like Anthony Trollope's Miss Thorne, whose "virtues were too numerous to describe, and not sufficiently interesting to deserve description."

We want a Christian faith that has stability but is not petrified; that has vision but is not hallucinatory. How do we get both the sense of stability and the spirit of adventure, the ballast of good health and the zest of true sanity? How do we get the adult maturity to keep our feet on the ground and retain the childlike innocence to make the leap of faith?

Psalm 132 is one of the oldest psalms in the Bible. It was included in the Psalms of Ascents to develop just those aspects of life under God and in Christ which my sometime friend Kelly lacked and which we all need.

It is a psalm of David's obedience, of "how he swore to the LORD and vowed to the Mighty One of Jacob." The psalm shows obedience as a lively, adventurous response of faith, that is rooted in historical fact and reaching into a promised hope.

Obedience with a History

The first half of Psalm 132 is the part that roots obedience in fact and keeps our feet on the ground. The psalm takes a single incident out of the past, the history of the ark of the covenant, and reminisces over it: "Lo, we heard of it in Ephrathah, we found it in the fields of Jaar. 'Let us go to his dwelling place; let us worship at his footstool!' Arise, O LORD, and go to thy resting place, thou and the ark of thy might."

The ark of the covenant was a box approximately forty-five inches long, twenty-seven inches broad and twenty-seven inches deep, constructed of wood and covered with gold. Its lid of solid gold was called the mercy seat. Two cherubim, angellike figures at either end, framed the space around the central mercy seat from which God's word was heard. It had been made under the supervision of Moses (Ex. 25:10-22) and was a symbol of the presence of God among his people. The ark had accompanied Israel from Sinai, through the wilderness wanderings, and had been kept at Shiloh from the time of the conquest. In a battle the ark had been captured by the enemy Philistines and was a trophy of war displayed in the Philistine cities until it became a problem to them (the story is told in 1 Samuel 4—7) and was returned to Israel to the village of Kiriath-jearim (7:1-2) where it rested until David came to get it and place it in honor in Jerusalem where it later became enshrined in Solomon's Temple.

The history of the ark was, for the Hebrews, a kind of theological handbook. It provided an account of the presence of God among the people. Its history showed the importance of having God with you and the danger of trying to use God or carry him around. And so the ark itself was important in that it emphasized that God was with his people, and that God was over and above his people (for God quite obviously was not in the box). The ark was the symbol not the reality. When the ark was treated as a talis-man, as a curio or as a magical device with which to manipu-late God, everything went wrong. God cannot be contained or used.

The psalm does not retell this history, it only remembers the history. There is only enough here to trigger the his-torical memories of the people. For the rich symbolism of the ark was everyday stuff to them. Its extensive and intri-cate history was common knowledge, much as the story of Jesus is to Christians. With promptings from the psalm the story would come alive for them again, especially the part that tells of the time that David rediscovered the ark in an obscure village and determined to set it at the center of Israelite life, restoring an old unity to the life of the people of God in adoration and worship. "Lo, we heard of it in Ephrathah, we found it in the fields of Jaar." News had come to David of where the ark was; he vowed to get it and was obedient to his vow. He gathered his people to himself and said: "Let us go to his dwelling place; let us worship at his footstool." He went to the ark and brought it up to Jerusalem in festive parade: "Arise, O LORD, and go to thy resting place, thou and the ark of thy might. Let thy priests be clothed with righteousness, and let thy saints shout for joy." As the song was sung we are told that "David danced before the LORD with all his might. . . . So David and all the house of Israel brought up the ark of the LORD with shouting, and with the sound of the horn" (2 Sam. 6: 14-15).

As this old ark song is resung now by the people of God on pilgrimage, historical memories are renovated and re-lived: there is a vast, rich reality of obedience beneath the feet of disciples. They are not the first persons to ascend these slopes on their way of obedience to God, and they will not be the last. Up these same roads, along these same paths, the ark had been carried, accompanied by a determined and expectant people. It had been carried in both good and bad ways. They would remember the time they carried it in panic ("I'm scared! Pray for me!"), super- stitiously as a secret weapon against the Philistines. *That* ended in calamity. They would also remember the Davidic parade of awed adoration and dancing celebration as obe- dience was turned into worship. Christians tramp well- worn paths: obedience has a history.

This history is important for without it we are at the mercy of whims. Memory is a data bank we use to evaluate our position and make decisions. With a biblical memory we have two thousand years of experience from which to make the off-the-cuff responses that are required each day in the life of faith. If we are going to live adequately and maturely as the people of God, we need more data to work from than our own experience can give us.

What would we think of a pollster who issued a definitive report on how the American people felt about a new tele- vision special, only to discover later that he had interviewed only one person who had seen only ten minutes of the program? We would dismiss the conclusions as frivolous. Yet that is exactly the kind of evidence that too many Christians accept as the final truth about many much more important matters—matters such as answered prayer, God's judgment, Christ's forgiveness, eternal salvation. The only person they consult is themselves and the only experience they evaluate is the most recent ten minutes. But we need other experiences, the community of experi- ence of brothers and sisters in the church, the centuries of experience provided by our biblical ancestors. A Christian who has David in his bones, Jeremiah in his bloodstream, Paul in his fingertips and Christ in his heart will know how much and how little value to put on his own momentary feelings and the experience of the past week.

To remain willfully ignorant of Abraham wandering in

the desert, the Hebrews enslaved in Egypt, David battling the Philistines, Jesus arguing with the Pharisees and Paul writing to the Corinthians is like saying, "I refuse to remember that when I kicked that black dog last week he bit my leg." If I don't remember it, in the next fit of anger I will kick him again and get bitten again. Biblical history is a good memory for what doesn't work. It is also a good memory for what does work—like remembering what you put in the soup that made it taste so good so that you can repeat and enjoy the recipe on another day; or remembering the short cut through the city to the ocean that saved you from being tied up in traffic and got you to the beach two hours earlier.

A Christian with a defective memory has to start everything from scratch and spends far too much of his or her time backtracking, repairing, starting over. A Christian with a good memory avoids repeating old sins, knows the easiest way through complex situations and instead of starting over each day continues what was begun in Adam. Psalm 132 activates faith's memory so that obedience will be sane. "Each act of obedience by the Christian is a modest proof, unequivocal for all its imperfection, of the reality of what he attests."[1]

Hope: A Race toward God's Promises

But Psalm 132 doesn't just keep our feet on the ground, it also gets them off the ground. It is not only a solid foundation in the past; it is a daring leap into the future. For obedience is not a stodgy plodding in the ruts of religion, it is a hopeful race toward God's promises. The second half of the psalm has a propellent quality to it. The psalmist is not an antiquarian, reveling in the past for its own sake, but a traveler using what he knows of the past to get to where he is going—to God.

For all its interest in history the Bible never refers to the past as "the good old times." The past is not, for the person of faith, a restored historical site that we tour when we are on vacation; it is a field that we plow and harrow and plant and fertilize and work for a harvest.

The second half of Psalm 132 takes seriously what God said to David and how David responded (matters that are remembered in the ark narrative) and uses them to make a vision of the reality that is in the future of faith: "I will abundantly bless her provisions; I will satisfy her poor with bread. Her priests I will clothe with salvation, and her saints will shout for joy. There I will make a horn to sprout for David; I have prepared a lamp for my anointed. His enemies I will clothe with shame, but upon himself his crown will shed its luster." All the verb tenses are future. Obedience is fulfilled by hope.

Now none of these hopes is unrelated to or detached from actual history: each develops from what a person with a good memory knows happened:

"I will abundantly bless her provisions; I will satisfy her poor with bread." The devout mind goes back to those years in the wilderness when God gave water from the rock, manna from the ground and quail from the skies, and fashions a hope for abundant, eternal providence.

"Her priests I will clothe with salvation, and her saints will shout for joy." No other people knew so much of salvation as Israel. The priests renewed the knowledge and applied it to daily life at every gathering of worship—occasions that were always marked with joy—renewing the life of redemption. Has any other people had such a good time with their faith as Israel? From Moses' song at the edge of the Red Sea with Miriam and the women accompanying with tambourines to the victorious trumpets that shook and finally tumbled the walls of Jericho, to the robust hymns of David that we continue to sing in our churches today, the joy has overflowed.

"There I will make a horn to sprout for David; I have prepared a lamp for my anointed." The horn was a sign of strength. The hope is that its brightness will provide light for the path of the one who represents God's presence, a light we now identify with revelation in Scripture and in Christ.

"His enemies I will clothe with shame, but upon himself his crown will shed its luster." The shame of God's enemies and the glory of God's king will finally be decisive. The triumph will be complete. Evil will lie sprawling in defeat, righteousness will flourish in victory. That is an agenda that hope writes for obedience.

Psalm 132 cultivates a hope that gives wings to obedience, a hope that is consistent with the reality of what God has done in the past but is not confined to it. All the expectations listed in Psalm 132 have their origin in an accurately remembered past. But they are not simply repetitions of the past projected into the future. They are developments *out* of it, with new features of their own.

Christians who master Psalm 132 will be protected from one danger, at least, that is ever a threat to obedience: the danger that we should reduce Christian existence to ritually obeying a few commandments that are congenial to our temperament and convenient to our standard of living. It gives us, instead, a vision into the future so that we can see what is right before us. If we define the nature of our lives by the mistake of the moment or the defeat of the hour or the boredom of the day, we will define it wrongly. We need roots in the past to give obedience ballast and breadth; we need a vision of the future to give obedience direction and goal. And they must be connected. There must be an organic unity between them. If we never learn how to do this, extend the boundaries of our lives beyond the dates enclosed by our birth and death and acquire an understanding of God's way as something larger and more complete than the anecdotes in our private diaries, we will forever be

missing the point of things by making headlines out of
something that ought to be tucked away on page 37 in section C of the newspaper, or putting into the classified ads
something that should be getting a full-page color adver-
tisement—mistaking a sore throat for a descent into hell.
("Peterson, pray for me!") For Christian faith cannot be
comprehended by examining an instamatic flash picture
which has caught a pose of beauty or absurdity, ecstasy or
terror; it is a full revelation of a vast creation and a grandly
consummated redemption. Obedience is doing what God
tells us to do in it.

The Strength to Stand; the Willingness to Leap

In such ways Psalm 132 cultivates the memory and nurtures
the hope that lead to mature obedience. It protects us from
a religion that is ignorant of the ways of God and so keeps
us prey to every fear that thrusts itself upon us. It guards us
from a religion riot with fantasies and nightmares because
it has gotten disassociated from the promises of God. It develops a strong sense of continuity with the past and a surg-
ing sense of exploration into the future. It is the kind of
thing we sing to stay normal without becoming dull, to walk
upright in the middle of the road without getting stuck in a
long rut of mediocrity. Its words prod us to reach into the
future without losing touch with daily reality. Its rhythms
stimulate us to new adventures in the Spirit without making
us lunatics. For Christian living demands that we keep our
feet on the ground; it also asks us to make a leap of faith.

A Christian who stays put is no better than a statue. A
person who leaps about constantly is under suspicion of being not a man but a jumping jack. What we require is obedience—the strength to stand and the willingness to leap,
and the sense to know when to do which. Which is exactly
what we get when an accurate memory of God's ways is
combined with a lively hope in his promises.

15: Community

"Like the Precious Oil upon the Head"

Behold, how good and pleasant it is
when brothers dwell in unity!
It is like the precious oil upon the head,
running down upon the beard,
upon the beard of Aaron,
running down on the collar of his robes!
It is like the dew of Hermon,
which falls on the mountains of Zion!
For there the LORD has commanded the blessing,
life for evermore.

Psalm 133

All actual life is encounter.

Martin Buber

Whether we like it or not, the moment we confess Jesus Christ as our Lord and Savior, that is, from the time we become a Christian, we are at the same time a member of the Christian church . . . even if we do not permit our name to be placed on a church roll, even if we refuse to identify ourselves with a particular congregation and share responsibilities with them, even if we absent ourselves from the worship of a congregation. Our membership in the church is a corollary of our faith in Christ. We can no more be a Christian and have nothing to do with the church than we can be a person and not be in a family. Membership in the church is a basic spiritual fact for those who confess Christ as Lord. It is not an option for those Christians who happen, by nature, to be more gregarious than others. It is part of the fabric of redemption.

There are Christians, of course, who never put their names down on a membership list; there are Christians who refuse to respond to the call to worship each Sunday; there are Christians who say, "I love God but I hate the church." But they are members all the same, whether they like it or not, whether they acknowledge it or not. For God never makes private, secret salvation deals with people. His relationships with us are personal, true: intimate, yes; but private, no. We are a family in Christ. When we become Christians, we are among brothers and sisters in faith. No Christian is an only child.

But, of course, just because we are a family of faith does not mean that we are one big happy family. The people we encounter as brothers and sisters in faith are not always nice people. They do not stop being sinners the moment they begin believing in Christ. They don't suddenly metamorphose into brilliant conversationalists, exciting companions and glowing inspirations. Some of them are cranky, some of them dull and others (if the truth must be spoken) a drag. But at the same time our Lord tells us that they are brothers and sisters in faith. If God is my father, then this is my family.

So the question is not, "Am I going to be a part of a community of faith?" but, "How am I going to live in this community of faith?" God's children do different things. Some run away from it and pretend that the family doesn't exist. Some move out and get an apartment on their own from which they return to make occasional visits, nearly always showing up for the parties and bringing a gift to show that they really do hold the others in fond regard. And some would never dream of leaving but cause others to dream it for them for they are always criticizing what is served at the meals, quarreling with the way the housekeeping is done and complaining that the others in the family are either ignoring or taking advantage of them. And some determine to find out what God has in mind by placing them in this community called a church, learn how to function in it harmoniously and joyously and develop the maturity that is able to share and exchange God's grace with those who might otherwise be viewed as nuisances.

Not Like Paying Taxes
Psalm 133 presents what we are after: "Behold, how good and pleasant it is when brothers dwell in unity!" The psalm puts into song what is said and demonstrated throughout Scripture and church: community is essential. Scripture knows nothing of the solitary Christian. People of faith are always members of a community. Creation itself was not complete until there was community, Adam needing Eve before humanity was whole. God never works with individuals in isolation, but always with people in community.

This is the biblical datum, and that with which we must

begin. Jesus worked with twelve disciples and lived with them in community. The church was formed when one hundred twenty people were "all together" in one place (Acts 2:1 and again in 5:12). When some early Christians were dropping out of the community and pursuing private interests, a pastor wrote to them urging them to nurture their precious gift of community, "not neglecting to meet together, as is the habit of some, but encouraging one another, and all the more as you see the Day drawing near" (Heb. 10:25). The Bible knows nothing of a religion that is defined by what a person does inwardly in the privacy of thought or feeling, or apart from others on lonely retreat. When Jesus was asked what the great commandment was, he said, "Love the Lord your God with all your heart, and with all your soul, and with all your mind," and then immediately, before anyone could go off and make a private religion out of it ("I come to the garden alone . . .") riveted it to another: "A second is like it, You shall love your neighbor as yourself" (Mt. 22:34-40).

Christians make this explicit in their act of worship each week by gathering as a community: other people are unavoidably present. As we come to declare our love for God we must face the unlovely and lovely fellow sinners whom God loves and commands us to love. This must not be treated as something to put up with, one of the inconvenient necessities of faith in the way that paying taxes is an inconvenient consequence of living in a secure and free nation. It is not only necessary; it is desirable that our faith have a social dimension, a human relationship: "Behold, how good and pleasant it is when brothers dwell in unity!"

For centuries this psalm was sung on the road as throngs of people made the ascent to Jerusalem for festival worship. Our imaginations readily reconstruct those scenes. How great to have everyone sharing a common purpose, traveling a common path, striving toward a common goal, that path and purpose and goal being God. How much better than making the long trip alone: "How good, how delightful it is for all to live together like brothers" (JB).

Two Ways to Avoid Community
But if living in community is necessary and desirable, it is also enormously difficult.[1] There is a clue to the nature of the difficulty in the simile "like brothers."

Most Christians have some firsthand experience of what it means to live "like brothers." Brothers fight. And sisters fight. The first story in the Bible about brothers living together is the story of Cain and Abel. And it is a murder story. Significantly, their fight was a religious fight, a quarrel over which of them God loved best. The story of Joseph and his brothers follows a few pages later, in which Joseph, envied by the rest, is sold into Egypt as a slave. David and his brothers fare no better and add to the evidence of discord. Even Jesus and his brothers are evidence of disharmony rather than peace. The one picture we have of them shows the brothers misunderstanding Jesus and trying to drag him away from his messianic work because they are convinced that he is crazy.

Those who have acquired their knowledge of human relationships by reading psychology books instead of the Bible find the case histories on this subject under the chapter entitled "Sibling Rivalry." But most of what is there is only a footnote to what Scripture says: children fight a lot; each brother is quick to take offense if he doesn't get his own way; each sister wants a major share of the parent's attention.

Children are ordinarily so full of their own needs and wants that they look at a brother or sister not as an ally but as a competitor. If there is only one pork chop on the plate and three of us who want it, I will no longer look at my brother and sister as delightful dinner companions but as difficult rivals. Much of the literature of the world (novels, plays, poetry) documents this: living together "like brothers" means, in actual practice, endless squabbles, murderous quarrels and angry arguments. And so if we are going to sing "how delightful it is for all to live together like brothers," we will not do it by being left to ourselves, following our natural bent. If we do, we will only get into a big fight, and the only delightful thing about it will be the pleasure the spectators get in watching us bloody each other's noses.

Living together in a way that evokes the glad song of Psalm 133 is one of the great and arduous tasks before Christ's people. Nothing requires more attention and energy. It is easier to do almost anything else. It is far easier to deal with people as problems to be solved than to have anything to do with them in community. If a person can be isolated from the family (from husband, from wife, from parents, from children, from neighbors) and then be professionally counseled, advised and guided without the complications of all of those relationships, things are very much simpler. But if such practices are engaged in systematically, they become an avoidance of community. Christians are a community of people who are visibly together at worship, but who remain in relationship through the week in witness and service. "In the beginning is the relation."[2]

Another common way to avoid community is to turn the church into an institution. In this way people are treated not on the basis of personal relationships but in terms of impersonal functions. Goals are set that will catch the imagination of the largest numbers of people; structures are developed that will accomplish the goal through planning and organization. Organizational planning and institutional goals become the criteria by which the community is defined and evaluated. In the process the church becomes less and less a community, that is, people who pay attention to each other, ("brothers living together"), and more and more a collectivism of "contributing units."

Every community of Christians is imperiled when either of these routes are pursued: the route of defining others as problems to be solved, the way one might repair an automobile; the route of lumping persons together in terms of economic ability or institutional effectiveness, the way one might run a bank. Somewhere between there is community —a place where each person is taken seriously, learns to trust others, depend on others, be compassionate with others, rejoice with others. "Behold, how good and pleasant it is when brothers dwell in unity!"

Each Other's Priest

There are two poetic images in Psalm 133 that are instinct with insights in the work of encouraging and shaping a good and delightful life together in Christ. The first image describes community as "precious oil upon the head, running down upon the beard, upon the beard of Aaron, running down on the collar of his robes!"

The picture comes from Exodus 29 where instructions are given for the ordination of Aaron and other priests. After sacrifices were prepared, Aaron was dressed in the priestly vestments. Then this direction is given: "you shall take the anointing oil, and pour it on his head and anoint him. . . . Thus you shall ordain Aaron and his sons" (Ex. 29:7, 9).

Oil, throughout Scripture, is a sign of God's presence, a symbol of the Spirit of God. The oil glistens, picks up the warmth of sunlight, softens the skin, perfumes the person. (Gerard Manley Hopkins, extolling God's grandeur in creation, uses a similar image in his line, "It gathers to a greatness, like the ooze of oil crushed."[3]) There is a quality of warmth and ease in God's community which contrasts with the icy coldness and hard surfaces of people who jostle each other in mobs and crowds.

But more particularly here the oil is an anointing oil, marking the person as a priest. Living together means seeing the oil flow over the head, down the face, through the beard, onto the shoulders of the other—and when I see that I know that my brother, my sister, is my priest. When we see the other as God's anointed, our relationships are profoundly affected.

No one has realized this more perceptively in our time than Dietrich Bonhoeffer. He wrote, "Not what a man is in himself as a Christian, his spirituality and piety, constitutes the basis of our community. What determines our brotherhood is what that man is by reason of Christ. Our community with one another consists solely in what Christ has done to both of us."[4] And what he has done is anoint us with his Spirit. We are set apart for service to one another. We mediate to one another the mysteries of God. We represent to one another the address of God. We are priests who speak God's Word and share Christ's sacrifice. "The Christian needs another Christian who speaks God's Word to him. He needs him again and again when he becomes uncertain and discouraged, for by himself he cannot help himself without belying the truth. He needs his brother man as a bearer and proclaimer of the divine word of salvation. He needs his brother solely because of Jesus Christ. The Christ in his own heart is weaker than the Christ in the word of his brother; his own heart is uncertain, his brother's is sure."[5]

In the second image, the community is "like the dew of Hermon, which falls on the mountains of Zion!" Hermon, the highest mountain in that part of the world, rose to a height of over nine thousand feet in the Lebanon range, north of Israel. Anyone who has slept overnight in high alpine regions knows how heavy the dew is at such altitudes. When you wake in the morning, you are drenched. This heavy dew, which was characteristic of each new dawn on the high slopes of Hermon is extended by the imagination to the hills of Zion—a copious dew, fresh and nurturing in the drier barren Judean country. The alpine dew communicates a sense of morning freshness, a feeling of fertility, a clean anticipation of growth.

Important in any community of faith is an ever-renewed sense of expectation in what God is doing with our brothers and sisters in the faith. We refuse to label the others as one thing or another. We refuse to predict our brother's behavior, our sister's growth. Each person in the community is unique, each is specially loved and particularly led by the Spirit of God. How can I presume to make conclusions about anyone? How can I pretend to know your worth or your place? Margaret Mead, who makes learned and passionate protests against the ways modern culture flattens out and demoralizes people, wrote, "No recorded cultural system has ever had enough different expectations to match all the children who were born within it."[6]

A community of faith flourishes when we view each other with this expectancy, wondering what God will do today in this one, in that one. When we are in a community with those Christ loves and redeems, we are constantly finding out new things about them. They are new persons each morning, endless in their possibilities. We explore the fascinating depths of their friendship, share the secrets of their quest. It is impossible to be bored in such a community, impossible to feel alienated among such people.

The oil flowing down Aaron's beard communicates a sense of warm, priestly relationship. The dew descending down Hermon's slopes communicates a sense of fresh and expectant newness. Oil and dew. The two things that make life together delightful.

Rousing Good Fellowship
The last line of the psalm concludes that the good and

delightful life together is where "the LORD has commanded the blessing, life for evermore."

Christians are always attempting and never quite succeed at getting a picture of the life everlasting. When we try to imagine it, we only banalize it. And then, having scrawled an uninteresting and amateurish sketch using the paint pots of an impoverished faith, we announce that we are not so sure we want to spend eternity in a place like that. Maybe we would prefer the rousing good fellowship of hell.

There is just a hint thrown out in Psalm 133 of heaven (a hint that is expanded into a grand vision in Revelation 4—5), that turns that on its head: the rousing good fellowship is in heaven. Where relationships are warm and expectancies fresh we are already beginning to enjoy the life together that will be completed in our life everlasting. Which means that heaven is like nothing quite so much as a good party. Assemble in your imagination all the friends that you enjoy being with most, the companions that evoke the deepest joy, your most stimulating relationships, the most delightful of shared experiences, the people with whom you feel completely alive—*that* is a hint at heaven, "for there the LORD has commanded the blessing, life for evermore."

April 9, 1945

One of the best, maybe *the* best, book written in this century on the meaning of living together as a family of faith is *Life Together* by Dietrich Bonhoeffer. The book begins with the words of the psalm, "Behold, how good and how pleasant it is for brethren to live together in unity!" The text was with Bonhoeffer all his life. His first publication, a doctoral dissertation at age twenty-one, was titled, "The Communion of the Saints." His book *The Cost of Discipleship* has been a handbook to a vast company of twentieth-century Christians on pilgrimage. During the Nazi years he led a fugitive community of seminarians, living with them in a daily quest to discover for themselves the meaning of being a family of faith in Christ and training them in the pastoral ministries that would lead others into that fellowship of a common life. It was during this period that he wrote *Life Together.*

During the last years of the Third Reich he was imprisoned by Adolph Hitler. But even then prison walls did not separate him from his brothers and sisters in Christ. He prayed for them and wrote letters to them, deepening the experience of community in Christ. And then he was killed. Even as his life had been an exploration of the first line of Psalm 133, his death was an exposition of the last line in which "the LORD has commanded the blessing, life for evermore."

The time was April 9th, 1945. The prison doctor at Flossenburg wrote this report: "On the morning of the day, some time between five and six o'clock the prisoners . . . were led out of their cells and the verdicts read to them. Through the half-open door of a room in one of the huts I saw Pastor Bonhoeffer, still in his prison clothes, kneeling in fervent prayer to the Lord his God. The devotion and evident conviction of being heard that I saw in the prayer of this intensely captivating man, moved me to the depths." So the morning came. Now the prisoners were ordered to strip. They were led down a little flight of steps under the trees to the secluded place of execution. There was a pause. . . . Naked under the scaffold in the sweet spring woods, Bonhoeffer knelt for the last time to pray. Five minutes later, his life was ended. . . . Three weeks later Hitler committed suicide. In another month the Third Reich had fallen. All Germany was in chaos and communications were impossible. No one knew what had happened to Bonhoeffer. His family waited in anguished uncertainty in Berlin. The report of his death was first received in Geneva and then telegraphed to England. On July 27th his aged parents, as was their custom turned on their radio to listen to the broadcast from London. A memorial service was in progress. The triumphant measures of Vaughan Williams' "For all the Saints" rolled out loud and solemn from many hundred voices. Then a single German was speaking in English, "We are gathered here in the presence of God to make thankful remembrance of the life and work of his servant Dietrich Bonhoeffer, who gave his life in faith and obedience to His holy word. . . . "[7]

In such a way one man showed in his life and death, even as we can in the communities we live in and lead, the rich and continuing truths of Psalm 133: "Behold, how good and pleasant it is when brothers dwell in unity! . . . For there the LORD has commanded the blessing, life for evermore."

16: Blessing
"Lift Up Your Hands"

Come, bless the LORD,
all you servants of the LORD,
who stand by night in the house of the LORD!
Lift up your hands to the holy place,
and bless the LORD!

May the LORD bless you from Zion,
he who made heaven and earth!

Psalm 134

Not seldom in this life; when, on the right side, fortune's favorites sail close by us, we, though all adroop before, catch somewhat of the rushing breeze, and joyfully feel our bagging sails fill out.

Herman Melville

The story Charles Colson tells of election night 1972 with President Nixon describes a familiar scene in the interior life of what could be anyone. There had been months of struggle, or strategy, of sacrifice. It had all paid off in a landslide victory. He was in the place that he had always wanted to be. The picture Colson draws of that night has three figures in it: Haldeman, arrogant and sullen; Nixon, restless and gulping Scotch; and Colson feeling let down, deflated, " . . . a deadness inside me." Three men at the power pinnacle of the world and not a single note of joy discernible in the room. "If someone had peered in on us that night from some imaginary peephole in the ceiling of the President's office, what a curious sight it would have been: a victorious President, grumbling over words he would grudgingly say to his fallen foe; his chief of staff angry, surly, and snarling; and the architect of his political strategy sitting in numbed stupor."[1]

The experience is not uncommon. We work hard for something, get it and then find we don't want it. We struggle for years to get to the top and find life there thoroughly boring. Colson wrote, "Being part of electing a President was the fondest ambition of my life. For three long years I had committed everything I had, every ounce of energy to Richard Nixon's cause. Nothing else mattered. We had had no time together as a family, no social life, no vacations."[2] And then, having in his hands what he had set out for, he found he couldn't enjoy it.

For some the goal is an academic degree; for some a career position; for some a certain standard of living; for some acquiring a possession, getting married, having a child, landing a job, visiting a country, meeting a celebrity. But having gotten what we had always wanted, we find that

we have not gotten what we wanted at all. We are less fulfilled than ever, and only conscious of "a deadness inside
me."

Stand, Stoop, Stay
In Psalm 120, the first of the Psalms of Ascents, we saw the
theme of *repentance* developed. The word in Hebrew is
t^e*shubah,* a turning away from the world and a turning
toward God; the initial move in a life-goal set on God. It was
addressed to the person at the crossroads, inviting each of
us to make the decision to set out on the way of faith. Each
of the psalms that followed has described a part of what
takes place along this pilgrim way among people who have
turned to God and follow him in Christ. We have discovered in these psalms beautiful lines, piercing insights,
dazzling truths, stimulating words. We have found that the
world in which these psalms are sung is a world of adventure and challenge, of ardor and meaning. We have realized that while there are certainly difficulties in the way of
faith, it cannot, by any stretch of the imagination, be called
dull. It requires everything that is in us; it enlists all our desires and abilities; it gathers our total existence into its
songs. But when we get to where we are going, what then?
What happens at the end of faith? What takes place when
we finally arrive? Will we be disappointed?

Psalm 134, the final Psalm of Ascents, provides the evidence. The way of discipleship that begins in an act of re-
pentance *(t*^e*shubah)* concludes in a life of praise *(b*^e*rakah).*
It doesn't take long to find the key word and controlling
thought in the psalm: *bless* the Lord, *bless* the Lord, the Lord
bless you.

There are two words which are translated "blessed" in
our Bibles. One is *ashre,* which describes the having-it-all-
together sense of well-being that comes when we are living
in tune with creation and redemption. It is what Psalm 1

announces and what Psalm 128 describes. It is what we experience when God blesses us. The word in Hebrew "is used only of men, never of God, (and) in the NT there are only two instances in which it is used of God *(makarios* in 1 Tim. 1:11; 6:15)."[3] The other word is *b^erakah*. It describes what God does to us and among us: he enters into covenant with us, he pours out his own life for us, he shares the goodness of his Spirit, the vitality of his creation, the joys of his redemption. He empties himself among us and we get what he is. That is *blessing.* When the first word is *t^eshubah* the last word is *b^erakah.*

God gets down on his knees among us; gets on our level and shares himself with us. He does not reside afar off and send us diplomatic messages, he kneels among us. That posture is characteristic of God. The discovery and realization of this is what defines what we know of God as *good news*—God shares himself generously and graciously. "Whichever form the blessing takes, it implies an exchange of the contents of the soul."[4] God enters into our need, he anticipates our goals, he "gets into our skin" and understands us better than we do ourselves. Everything we learn about God through Scripture and in Christ tells us that he knows what it is like to change a diaper for the thirteenth time in the day, have a report over which we have worked long and carefully gather dust on somebody's desk for weeks and weeks, find our teaching treated with scorn and indifference by children and youth, discover that the integrity and excellence of our work has been overlooked and the shoddy duplicity of another's rewarded with a promotion. A book on God has for its title *The God Who Stands, Stoops, and Stays.* That summarizes the posture of blessing: God stands—he is foundational and dependable; God stoops—he kneels to our level and meets us where we are; God stays—he sticks with us through hard times and good, sharing his life with us in grace and peace.

And because God blesses us, we bless God. We respond with that which we have received. We participate in the process which God has initiated and continues. We who are blessed, bless. When the word is used for what people do, it has, in Scripture, the sense of "praise and gratitude for blessing received."[5] The people who learn what it is like to receive the blessing, persons who travel the way of faith experiencing the ways of grace in all kinds of weather and over every kind of terrain, become good at blessing. In Israel this became "the distinctive expression of the practice of religion."[6] In Judaism to this day all forms of prayer which begin with praise of God are called *berakoth,* that is, blessings.[7]

An Invitation and a Command

There is no better summarizing and concluding word in all of Scripture than the word *blessing.* It describes what we most prize in God's dealing with us and what is most attractive when we evaluate our way of living. Every act of worship concludes with a benediction. Psalm 134 features the word in a form that might be called an invitational command: "Come, bless the LORD. . . . Lift up your hands . . . and bless the LORD!"

The persons who first sang this song had been traveling, literally, the roads that led to Jerusalem. Now they had arrived and were at the temple to worship God in festival celebration. Some would have been on the road for days, some for weeks, in some instances, perhaps, for months. Now they were at the end of the road. What will happen? What will they feel? What will they do? Will there be the "deadness inside"?

Read in one way the sentence is an invitation: "Come, bless the LORD." The great promise of being in Jerusalem is that all might join in the rich temple worship. You are welcome now to do it. Come and join in. Don't be shy. Don't hold back. Did you have a fight with your wife on the way? That's all right. You are here now. Bless the Lord. Did you quarrel with your neighbor while making the trip? Forget it. You are here now. Bless the Lord. Did you lose touch with your children while coming and aren't sure just where they are now? Put that aside for the moment. They have their own pilgrimage to make. You are here. Bless the Lord. Are you ashamed of the feelings you had while traveling? the grumbling you indulged in? the resentment you harbored? Well, it wasn't bad enough to keep you from arriving, and now that you are here, bless the Lord. Are you embarassed at the number of times you quit and had to have someone pick you up and carry you along? No matter. You are here. Bless the Lord.

The sentence is an invitation; it is also a command. Having arrived at the place of worship, will we now sit around and tell stories about the trip? Having gotten to the big city, will we spend our time here as tourists, visiting the bazaars, window-shopping and trading? Having gotten Jerusalem checked off of our list of things to do, will we immediately begin looking for another challenge, another holy place to visit? Will the Temple be a place to socialize, receive congratulations from others on our achievement, a place to share gossip and trade stories, a place to make business contacts that will improve our prospects back home? But that is not why you made the trip: bless the Lord. You are here because the Lord blessed you. Now you bless the Lord.

Our stories may be interesting but they are not the point. Our achievements may be marvelous but they are not germane. Our curiosity may be understandable but it is not relevant. Bless the Lord. "When the perfect comes, the imperfect will pass away" (1 Cor. 13:10). Bless the Lord. Do that for which you were created and redeemed; lift your voices in gratitude; enter into the community of praise and prayer that anticipates the final consummation of faith in heaven. Bless the Lord.

Feelings Don't Run the Show

We are invited to bless the Lord; we are commanded to bless the Lord. And then someone says, "But I don't feel like it. And I won't be a hypocrite. I can't bless the Lord if I don't feel like blessing the Lord. It wouldn't be honest."

The biblical response to that is, "Lift up your hands to the holy place, and bless the LORD!" You can lift up your hands regardless of how you feel; it is a simple motor movement. You may not be able to command your heart, but you can command your arms. Lift your arms in blessing; just maybe your heart will get the message and be lifted up also in praise. We are psychosomatic beings; body and spirit are intricately interrelated. Go through the motions of blessing God and your spirit will pick up the cue and follow along. "For why do men lift their hands when they pray? Is it not that their hearts may be raised at the same time to God?"[8]

It isn't quite the same thing, and there are many differences in detail, but there is a broad similarity between the directions in the psalm and the contemporary movement known as "behavior modification"—which in a rough-and-ready way means that you can act yourself into a new way of being. Find the right things to do, practice the actions and other things will follow. "Lift up your hands to the holy place, and bless the LORD." Act your gratitude; pantomime your thanks; you will become that which you do.

Many think that the only way to change your behavior is to first change your feelings. We take a pill to alter our moods so that we won't kick the dog. We turn on music to soothe our emotions so that our conversation will be less abrasive. But there is an older wisdom that puts it differently: by changing our behavior we can change our feelings. One person says, "I don't like that man; therefore I will not speak to him. When and if my feelings change, I will speak."

Another says, "I don't like that person; therefore I am going to speak to him." The person, surprised at the friendliness, cheerfully responds and suddenly friendliness is shared. One person says, "I don't feel like worshiping; therefore I am not going to church. I will wait till I feel like it and then I will go." Another says, "I don't feel like worshiping; therefore I will go to church and put myself in the way of worship." In the process she finds herself blessed and begins, in turn, to bless.

Most probably the people who were first addressed by this command were the professional leaders of worship in the Jerusalem Temple, the Levites ("who stand by night in the house of the LORD"). They worked in shifts around the clock during festival time, and through the night some of them were always on duty. The great danger in those hours was that the worship be listless and slovenly. "What can you expect at three o'clock in the morning." "No excuses," says the psalm singer, "your feelings might be flat but you can control your muscles: lift up your hands." Humphrey Bogart once defined a professional as a person who "did a better job when he didn't feel like it." That goes for a Christian too. Feelings don't run the show. There is a reality deeper than our feelings. Live by that. Eric Routley thinks that, colloquially, to bless means to "speak well of."[9] The Lord has spoken well of you; now you speak well of him.

Taking God Seriously but Not Ourselves
It is as easy to find instances of people who bless in Christian ranks as it is to find examples of people who curse in the world's.

Karl Barth is one of my favorites. He is one of the great theologians of all time, but the really attractive thing about him is that he was a man who blessed God. His mind was massive, his learning immense, his theological industry simply staggering. He wrote a six-million-word, seven-thousand-page, twelve-volume dogmatics plus forty or fifty other books and several hundred learned articles. Impressive as that is, what is far more impressive, to me at least, is what he called *dankbarkeit.* Gratitude. Always and everywhere we are aware that Barth was responding to God's grace; there is a chuckle rumbling underneath his most serious prose; there is a twinkle on the edges of his eyes—always. He never took himself seriously and always took God seriously and therefore was full of cheerfulness, exuberant with blessing. Speaking of his own work as a theologian he said, "The theologian who has no joy in his work is not a theologian at all. Sulky faces, morose thoughts and boring ways of speaking are intolerable in this science."[10]

He was on a bus in Basel, the Swiss city in which he lived and taught for so many years. A man came and sat beside him, a tourist. Barth struck up a conversation, "You are a visitor, yes? And what do you want to see in our city?" The man said, "I would like to see the great theologian, Karl Barth. Do you know him?" "Oh, yes," said Barth, "I shave him every morning." The man went away satisfied, telling his friends that he had met Barth's barber.

Because he refused to take himself seriously and decided to take God seriously he burdened neither himself nor those around him with the gloomy, heavy seriousness of ambition or pride or sin or self-righteousness. Instead, the lifting up of hands, the brightness of blessing.

Charles Dickens described one of his characters as a person "who called her rigidity religion."[11] We find that kind of thing far too often, but, thankfully, we do not find it in Scripture. In Scripture we find Jesus concluding his parable of the lost sheep with the words, "I tell you, there will be more joy in heaven over one sinner who repents" (Lk. 15:7). Not relief, not surprise, not self-satisfied smugness. And certainly not the "deadness inside me." But joy. Blessing is at the end of the road. And that which is at the end of the road influences everything that takes place along the road. The end shapes the means. As Catherine of Siena said, "All the way to heaven is heaven." A joyful end requires a joyful means. Bless the Lord.

The Chief End

I have a friend who is dean in a theological seminary where men and women are being trained to be pastors. Sometimes he calls one of these people into his office and says something like this: "You have been around here for several months now and I have had an opportunity to observe you. You get good grades, seem to take your calling to ministry seriously, work hard and have clear goals. But I don't detect any joy. You don't seem to have any pleasure in what you are doing. And I wonder if you should not reconsider your calling into ministry. For if a pastor is not in touch with joy, it will be difficult to teach or preach convincingly that the news is good. If you do not convey joy in your demeanor and gestures and speech, you will not be an authentic witness for Jesus Christ. Delight in what God is doing is essential in our work."

The first question in the Westminster Shorter Catechism is "What is the chief end of man?" What is the final purpose? What is the main thing about us? Where are we going, and what will we do when we get there? The answer is, "To glorify God and enjoy him forever."

Glorify. Enjoy. There are other things involved in Christian discipleship. The Psalms of Ascents have shown some of them. But it is extremely important to know the one thing that overrides everything else. The main thing is not work for the Lord; it is not suffering in the name of the Lord; it is not witnessing to the Lord; it is not teaching Sunday school for the Lord; it is not being responsible for the sake of the Lord in the community; it is not keeping the Ten Commandments; not loving your neighbor; not observing the golden rule. "The chief end of man is to glorify God and enjoy him forever." Or, in the vocabulary of Psalm 134, "Bless the LORD."

"*Charis* always demands the answer *eucharistia* (that is, grace always demands the answer of gratitude). Grace and gratitude belong together like heaven and earth. Grace evokes gratitude like the voice an echo. Gratitude follows grace as thunder follows lightning."[12] God is personal reality to be enjoyed. We are so created and so redeemed that we are capable of enjoying him. All the movements of discipleship arrive at a place where joy is experienced. Every step of assent toward God develops the capacity to enjoy. Not only is there, increasingly, more to be enjoyed, there is steadily the acquired ability to enjoy it.

Best of all, we don't have to wait until we get to the end of the road before we enjoy what is at the end of the road. So, "Come, bless the LORD. . . . The LORD bless you!"

May it be our blessedness, as years go on, to add one grace to another, and advance upward, step by step, neither neglecting the lower after attaining the higher, nor aiming at the higher before attaining the lower. The first grace is faith, the last is love; first comes zeal, afterwards comes loving-kindness; first comes humiliation, then comes peace; first comes diligence, then comes resignation. May we learn to mature all graces in us; fearing and trembling, watching and repenting, because Christ is coming; joyful, thankful, and careless of the future, because he is come.[13]

Notes

Chapter 1

[1] *The Book of Common Prayer* (New York: The Church Pension Fund, 1945), p. 276.

[2] Amos T. Wilder writes, "World means more than 'mankind fallen away from God.' . . . The world is created and loved by God, and Christ has come to save it. But it is ephemeral, subject to decay and death; moreover, it has fallen under the control of the evil one, and therefore into darkness." *The Interpreter's Bible,* ed. George Arthur Buttrick (Nashville: Abingdon, 1952), XII, 238.

[3] Gore Vidal, *Matters of Fact and Fiction* (New York: Random House, 1977), p. 86.

[4] Friedrich Nietzsche, *Beyond Good and Evil,* trans. Helen Zimmern (London: 1907), Section 188, pp. 106-9.

[5] There is no independent documentation that the Psalms of Ascents were used thus, and therefore no consensus among scholars that they were associated with the pilgrimage journeys to Jerusalem. The connection is conjectural but not at all fanciful. Commentators, both Jewish and Christian, have interpreted these psalms in this framework.

[6] Paul Tournier, *A Place for You* (New York: Harper & Row, 1968), p. 163.

[7] Thomas Szasz, *Schizophrenia, The Sacred Symbol of Psychiatry* (Garden City: Doubleday, 1978), p. 72.

[8] Paul Goodman, *Little Prayers and Finite Experience* (New York: Harper & Row, 1972), p. 16.

[9] William Faulkner, quoted in Sam di Bonaventura's Program Notes to Elie Siegmeister's Symphony No. 5, Baltimore Symphony Concert, May 5, 1977.

Chapter 2

[1] John Baillie, *Invitation to Pilgrimage* (New York: Chas. Scribner's and Sons, 1942), p. 8.

[2] Elie Weisel, *Souls on Fire* (New York: Vintage, 1973), p. 154.

[3] Abraham Heschel, *The Prophets* (New York: Harper & Row, 1962), pp. 71-72.

[4] Ibid., p. 190.

Chapter 3

[1] John Calvin, *Commentary on the Psalms* (Grand Rapids, Mich.: Eerdmans, 1949), V, 63.

[2] Johannes Pedersen describes the situation thus: "The sun and the moon, which meant so much for the maintenance of order in life,

often became independent gods among the neighboring peoples or became part of the nature of other gods. Job expressly denies having kissed his hand to these mighty beings ('... if I have looked at the sun when it shone, or the moon moving in splendor, and my heart has been secretly enticed, and my mouth has kissed my hand; this also would be an iniquity to be punished by the judgment, for I should have been false to God above'). And in a judgment prophecy it is said that Yahweh will visit all the host of heaven on high, and the kings on earth, and the sun and the moon shall be put to shame, when Yahweh shall reign in Zion ('Then the moon shall be confounded and the sun ashamed; for the Lord of hosts will reign on Mount Zion and in Jerusalem.' Isaiah 24:33)." *Israel, Its Life and Culture* (London: Oxford University Press, 1926), III-IV, 635.

[3] There are, of course, numerous instances when hills and mountains are used as a metaphor for the strength and majesty of God; for instance, Ps. 3:4; 24:3; 43:3; 48:1.

Chapter 4
[1] Paul Scherer, *The Word God Sent* (New York: Harper & Row, 1965), p. 166.
[2] Herbert Hendin, *The Age of Sensation* (New York: Norton, 1975), p. 325.
[3] Charles Spurgeon, quoted in H. Thielicke, *Encounter with Spurgeon* (Philadelphia: Fortress, 1963), p. 11.

Chapter 5
[1] Walther Zimmerli, *"charis,"* in Gerhard Kittel, ed., *Theological Dictionary of the New Testament,* IX (Grand Rapids: Eerdmans, 1974), 377.

Chapter 6
[1] Robert Browning, "Easter Day," in *The Poems and Plays of Robert Browning* (New York: Random House, 1934), p. 503.

Chapter 7
[1] George Adam Smith, *Historical Geography of the Holy Land* (London: Collins, 1966), p. 178.
[2] Gilbert Highet, *Man's Unconquerable Mind* (New York: Columbia University Press, 1954), p. 24.
[3] Alexander Maclaren, *The Psalms* (New York: A. C. Armstrong and Son, 1908), II, 316.
[4] A better translation is that by Mitchell Dahood: "But those tottering for their devious ways. . . ." By repointing the Hebrew consonants he finds the psalmist using the same word as in verse 1 *(mwt)* and so contrasting the one who trusts in God and is "not moved" with the one who refused to trust in God and therefore "totters." *Psalms III* (Garden City: Doubleday, 1970), p. 214.

[5]Charles Spurgeon, *The Treasury of David* (Grand Rapids, Mich.: Zondervan, 1950), VI, 59.

Chapter 8

[1]Ellen Glasgow, *The Woman Within* (New York: Harcourt, Brace and Co., 1954), p. 15.
[2]Phyllis McGinley, *Saint-Watching* (New York: Viking, 1969), pp. 113-14.
[3]Elie Weisel, p. 100.

Chapter 9

[1]Hilary of Tours, quoted in G. A. Studdert-Kennedy, *The Word and The Work* (London: Hodder and Stoughton, 1965), p. 33.

Chapter 10

[1]Two Hebrew words are translated "blessed" in this psalm. The word used in verses 1-2 *('ašre)* describes the sense of happiness and wholeness that comes from living in good relationship with God. The word used in verses 4-5 *(barak)* describes what God does as he shares his abundant life with us in a relationship of salvation.
[2]F. Hauck, *"makarios,"* in *Theological Dictionary of the New Testament,* IV (1967), 369.
[3]Pedersen, I, 182-99.
[4]Ibid., pp. 193, 211.
[5]Calvin, V, 115.
[6]Austin Farrer, *The Brink of Mystery* (London: SPCK, 1976), p. 52.
[7]W. D. White, ed., *The Preaching of John Henry Newman* (Philadelphia: Fortress, 1969), p. 77.

Chapter 11

[1]H. Cremer, quoted in Gerhard von Rad, *Theology of the Old Testament* (New York: Harper & Row, 1962), I, 371.

Chapter 12

[1]Sally Cunneen, "Listening to Illich," *The Christian Century,* 29 Sept. 1976.
[2]P. T. Forsyth, *The Cure of Souls* (Grand Rapids, Mich.: Eerdmans, 1971), p. 128.
[3]Von Rad, I, 384.
[4]Henri J. M. Nouwen, *The Wounded Healer* (New York: Doubleday, 1972), p. 95.
[5]George MacDonald, *Unspoken Sermons, First Series,* quoted in frontispiece of C. S. Lewis, *The Problem of Pain* (New York: Macmillan, 1953).
[6]Forsyth, p. 113.
[7]Karl Barth, *Church Dogmatics* (Edinburgh: T. & T. Clark, 1957), II/1,

369.

[8] George MacDonald quoted in Denis Donogue, *New York Review of Books*, 21 Dec. 1967.

[9] Augustine, *The City of God* (New York: Doubleday, 1958), p. 46.

Chapter 13

[1] Gilbert Keith Chesterton, *Orthodoxy* (New York: John Lane, 1909), p. 212.

[2] Calvin, V, 140.

[3] Artur Weiser, *The Psalms* (Philadelphia: Westminster, 1962), p. 777.

[4] Spurgeon, VI, 137.

[5] Ibid., p. 136.

[6] Peter Marin, *Saturday Review of Literature*, 19 Sept. 1970, p. 73.

Chapter 14

[1] Barth, IV/3, second half, 670.

Chapter 15

[1] Philip Slater, in his searching study of the way Americans live together says that all of us have a desire and need for community—"the wish to live in trust and fraternal cooperation with one's fellows in a total and visible collective entity. It is easy to produce examples of the many ways in which Americans attempt to minimize, circumvent, or deny the interdependence upon which all human societies are based. We seek a private house, a private means of transportation, a private garden, a private laundry, self-service stores, and do-it-yourself skills of every kind. An enormous technology seems to have set itself the task of making it unnecessary for one human being ever to ask anything of another in the course of going about his daily business... we seek more and more privacy, and feel more and more alienated and lonely when we get it... our encounters with others tend increasingly to be competitive as a result of the search for privacy. We less and less often meet our fellow man to share and exchange, and more and more often encounter him as an impediment or a nuisance: making the highway crowded when we are rushing somewhere, cluttering and littering the beach or park or wood, pushing in front of us at the supermarket, taking the last parking place, polluting our air and water, building a highway through our house, blocking our view, and so on. Because we have cut off so much communication with each other we keep bumping into each other, and thus a higher and higher percentage of our interpersonal contacts are abrasive." *Pursuit of Loneliness* (Boston: Beacon, 1970), pp. 7-8.

[2] Martin Buber, *I and Thou* (New York: Charles Scribner's Sons, 1970), p. 62.

[3]*Poems and Prose of Gerard Manley Hopkins* (Baltimore: Penguin, 1953), p. 27.

[4]Dietrich Bonhoeffer, *Life Together* (New York: Harper and Brothers, 1954), p. 25.

[5]Ibid., p. 23.

[6]Margaret Mead, *Culture and Commitment* (Garden City: Natural History Press/Doubleday, 1970), p. 17.

[7]Mary Bosenquet, *The Life and Death of Dietrich Bonhoeffer* (New York: Harper & Row, 1968), pp. 15-16.

Chapter 16

[1]Charles Colson, *Born Again* (New York: Bantam Books, 1976), p. 10.

[2]Ibid., p. 7.

[3]George Arthur Buttrick, ed., *Interpreter's Dictionary of the Bible* (Nashville: Abingdon, 1962), I, 445.

[4]Pedersen, I-II, 202.

[5]*Interpreter's Dictionary,* I, 446.

[6]B. Duhm, *Das Buch Hiob* (1897), p. 12, quoted in Hermann W. Beyer, *"eulogeō,"* in *Theological Dictionary of the New Testament,* II (1964), 758.

[7]Ibid., p. 760.

[8]Calvin, p. 168.

[9]Eric Routley, *Ascent to the Cross* (London: SCM Press Ltd., 1962), p. 72.

[10]Barth, II/1, 656.

[11]Charles Dickens, *Great Expectations* (New York: Heritage, 1939), p. 198.

[12]Barth, IV/1, 41.

[13]John Henry Newman, *The Preaching of John Henry Newman,* ed. W. E. White (Philadelphia: Fortress Press, 1969), p. 211.